50 Restaurant Baking Recipes for Home

By: Kelly Johnson

Table of Contents

- Classic Chocolate Chip Cookies
- New York Style Cheesecake
- French Baguettes
- Blueberry Muffins
- Red Velvet Cupcakes
- Lemon Bars
- Cinnamon Rolls
- Apple Pie
- Raspberry Almond Scones
- Chocolate Lava Cake
- Buttermilk Biscuits
- Key Lime Pie
- Carrot Cake with Cream Cheese Frosting
- Pecan Pie Bars
- Italian Cannoli
- Banana Bread
- Flourless Chocolate Cake
- Pumpkin Spice Latte Cupcakes
- Almond Croissants
- Tiramisu
- Chocolate Eclairs
- Maple Pecan Cinnamon Rolls
- Strawberry Shortcake
- Peanut Butter Blossom Cookies
- Classic Eclairs
- Chocolate Babka
- Linzer Cookies
- Almond Joy Brownies
- Lemon Poppy Seed Muffins
- Black Forest Cake
- Snickerdoodle Cookies
- Coconut Cream Pie
- Hazelnut Macarons
- Puff Pastry Palmiers
- S'mores Brownies

- Apple Cider Donuts
- Mint Chocolate Chip Ice Cream Sandwiches
- Peanut Butter Cupcakes
- Cranberry Orange Scones
- Dark Chocolate Torte
- Raspberry Swirl Cheesecake Bars
- Classic Danish Pastry
- Pistachio Baklava
- Strawberry Rhubarb Pie
- Chocolate Cherry Tart
- Lemon Lavender Shortbread Cookies
- Vanilla Bean Madeleines
- Chocolate Hazelnut Biscotti
- Raspberry Chocolate Ganache Tart
- Oatmeal Raisin Cookies

Classic Chocolate Chip Cookies

Ingredients:

- 1 cup (2 sticks) unsalted butter, softened
- 3/4 cup granulated sugar
- 3/4 cup packed brown sugar
- 2 large eggs
- 1 teaspoon vanilla extract
- 2 1/4 cups all-purpose flour
- 1 teaspoon baking soda
- 1/2 teaspoon salt
- 2 cups semisweet chocolate chips
- 1 cup chopped nuts (optional)

Instructions:

Preheat the Oven:
- Preheat your oven to 375°F (190°C). Line baking sheets with parchment paper.

Cream Butter and Sugars:
- In a large mixing bowl, cream together the softened butter, granulated sugar, and brown sugar until light and fluffy.

Add Eggs and Vanilla:
- Add the eggs one at a time, beating well after each addition. Stir in the vanilla extract.

Combine Dry Ingredients:
- In a separate bowl, whisk together the all-purpose flour, baking soda, and salt.

Combine Wet and Dry Ingredients:
- Gradually add the dry ingredients to the wet ingredients, mixing just until combined. Be careful not to overmix.

Add Chocolate Chips and Nuts:
- Fold in the chocolate chips and chopped nuts (if using) until evenly distributed throughout the cookie dough.

Scoop Dough onto Baking Sheets:
- Drop rounded tablespoons of dough onto the prepared baking sheets, leaving enough space between each cookie.

Bake:
- Bake in the preheated oven for 9-11 minutes or until the edges are golden brown. The centers may still look slightly soft.

Cool:
- Allow the cookies to cool on the baking sheets for a few minutes before transferring them to wire racks to cool completely.

Enjoy:
- Once cooled, enjoy your classic chocolate chip cookies with a glass of milk or your favorite beverage!

Feel free to adjust the chocolate chip and nut quantities based on your preferences.

Happy baking!

New York Style Cheesecake

Ingredients:

For the Crust:

- 2 cups graham cracker crumbs
- 1/2 cup unsalted butter, melted
- 1/4 cup granulated sugar

For the Filling:

- 4 packages (8 ounces each) cream cheese, softened
- 1 1/4 cups granulated sugar
- 1 cup sour cream
- 1 teaspoon vanilla extract
- 4 large eggs

For the Topping (optional):

- 1 cup sour cream
- 2 tablespoons granulated sugar
- 1 teaspoon vanilla extract

Instructions:

For the Crust:

Preheat your oven to 325°F (163°C). Grease a 9-inch springform pan. In a medium bowl, combine the graham cracker crumbs, melted butter, and sugar. Press the mixture into the bottom of the prepared pan to form the crust. Bake the crust in the preheated oven for 10 minutes. Remove from the oven and let it cool while preparing the filling.

For the Filling:

In a large mixing bowl, beat the softened cream cheese until smooth.
Add the granulated sugar and beat until well combined.
Mix in the sour cream and vanilla extract until smooth.
Add the eggs, one at a time, beating well after each addition. Scrape down the sides of the bowl as needed.
Pour the cream cheese mixture over the cooled crust in the springform pan.
Bake in the preheated oven for 55-65 minutes or until the edges are set, and the center is slightly jiggly. The top should be lightly golden.
Turn off the oven and leave the cheesecake in the oven for 1 hour to cool gradually. This helps prevent cracking.
Remove the cheesecake from the oven and let it cool completely. Refrigerate for at least 4 hours or overnight before adding the optional topping.

For the Topping (optional):

In a small bowl, mix together the sour cream, sugar, and vanilla extract.
Spread the sour cream mixture over the chilled cheesecake.
Return the cheesecake to the refrigerator for an additional 1-2 hours to set the topping.
Once fully chilled and set, run a knife around the edges of the pan before releasing the springform.

Slice and enjoy your classic New York Style Cheesecake!

French Baguettes

Ingredients:

- 4 cups all-purpose flour
- 1 tablespoon sugar
- 1 tablespoon active dry yeast
- 1 1/2 teaspoons salt
- 1 1/2 cups warm water (about 110°F/43°C)
- Cornmeal, for dusting

Instructions:

Activate the Yeast:
- In a small bowl, combine warm water and sugar. Stir until the sugar dissolves. Sprinkle the yeast over the water and let it sit for about 5-10 minutes until it becomes frothy.

Prepare the Dough:
- In a large mixing bowl, combine the flour and salt. Make a well in the center and pour in the activated yeast mixture.

Knead the Dough:
- Gradually incorporate the flour into the wet ingredients until a dough forms. Transfer the dough to a floured surface and knead for about 10 minutes until it becomes smooth and elastic.

First Rise:
- Place the dough in a lightly oiled bowl, cover it with a damp cloth, and let it rise in a warm place for 1-2 hours or until it has doubled in size.

Shape the Baguettes:
- Turn the dough onto a floured surface and divide it into two equal portions. Shape each portion into a rectangle, then roll it up tightly from the long side to form a baguette shape.

Second Rise:
- Place the shaped baguettes on a parchment-lined baking sheet sprinkled with cornmeal. Cover them with a damp cloth and let them rise for another 30-45 minutes.

Preheat the Oven:
- Preheat your oven to 450°F (230°C). Place a pan of water on the bottom rack of the oven to create steam, which helps develop a crispy crust.

Score the Baguettes:
- Using a sharp knife or a razor blade, make diagonal slashes (score) on the top of each baguette.

Bake:
- Bake in the preheated oven for 20-25 minutes or until the baguettes are golden brown and sound hollow when tapped.

Cool:
- Allow the baguettes to cool on a wire rack before slicing.

Enjoy your homemade French baguettes with your favorite spreads, cheeses, or as a side for soups and salads!

Blueberry Muffins

Ingredients:

- 1 1/2 cups all-purpose flour
- 3/4 cup granulated sugar
- 1/2 teaspoon salt
- 2 teaspoons baking powder
- 1/3 cup vegetable oil
- 1 large egg
- 1/3 cup milk (you can use buttermilk for a richer flavor)
- 1 1/2 teaspoons vanilla extract
- 1 1/2 cups fresh or frozen blueberries

Instructions:

Preheat your oven to 400°F (200°C). Line a muffin tin with paper liners or grease the cups.

In a large mixing bowl, whisk together the flour, sugar, salt, and baking powder.

In a separate bowl, mix together the vegetable oil, egg, milk, and vanilla extract.

Add the wet ingredients to the dry ingredients and stir until just combined. Be careful not to overmix; a few lumps are okay.

Gently fold in the blueberries until evenly distributed throughout the batter.

Spoon the batter into the prepared muffin cups, filling each about two-thirds full.

Bake in the preheated oven for 18-20 minutes or until a toothpick inserted into the center of a muffin comes out clean or with just a few crumbs.

Allow the muffins to cool in the tin for a few minutes, then transfer them to a wire rack to cool completely.

Enjoy your homemade blueberry muffins! Feel free to customize the recipe by adding a streusel topping, lemon zest, or other ingredients to suit your taste.

Red Velvet Cupcakes

Ingredients:

For the cupcakes:

- 1 1/4 cups all-purpose flour
- 1/2 teaspoon baking powder
- 1/2 teaspoon baking soda
- 1/4 teaspoon salt
- 2 tablespoons unsweetened cocoa powder
- 3/4 cup granulated sugar
- 1/2 cup vegetable oil
- 2 large eggs
- 1 teaspoon vanilla extract
- 1/2 cup buttermilk
- 1 tablespoon red food coloring (adjust to achieve desired color)

For the cream cheese frosting:

- 8 ounces cream cheese, softened
- 1/2 cup unsalted butter, softened
- 2 cups powdered sugar
- 1 teaspoon vanilla extract

Instructions:

Preheat your oven to 350°F (175°C). Line a muffin tin with cupcake liners.
In a medium bowl, whisk together the flour, baking powder, baking soda, salt, and cocoa powder.
In a large bowl, beat together the sugar and vegetable oil until well combined.
Add the eggs one at a time, beating well after each addition. Stir in the vanilla extract.
In a small bowl, combine the buttermilk and red food coloring.
Add the dry ingredients to the sugar mixture in three additions, alternating with the buttermilk mixture. Begin and end with the dry ingredients, mixing until just combined.

Divide the batter evenly among the cupcake liners, filling each about two-thirds full.

Bake for 18-20 minutes or until a toothpick inserted into the center of a cupcake comes out clean.

Allow the cupcakes to cool in the tin for a few minutes before transferring them to a wire rack to cool completely.

For the cream cheese frosting, beat together the cream cheese, butter, powdered sugar, and vanilla extract until smooth and creamy.

Once the cupcakes are completely cooled, frost them with the cream cheese frosting using a piping bag or a spatula.

These Red Velvet Cupcakes are sure to be a hit at any gathering or celebration!

Lemon Bars

Ingredients:

For the crust:

- 1 cup unsalted butter, softened
- 1/2 cup granulated sugar
- 2 cups all-purpose flour
- 1/4 teaspoon salt

For the lemon filling:

- 2 cups granulated sugar
- 1/4 cup all-purpose flour
- 4 large eggs
- 2/3 cup fresh lemon juice (about 4-5 lemons)
- Zest of 2 lemons
- Powdered sugar for dusting (optional)

Instructions:

Preheat your oven to 350°F (175°C). Grease a 9x13-inch baking pan or line it with parchment paper, leaving some overhang for easy removal.
In a large bowl, cream together the softened butter and granulated sugar until light and fluffy. Add the flour and salt, and mix until the dough comes together.
Press the dough evenly into the bottom of the prepared baking pan. Use the back of a spoon or your hands to create a smooth, even crust.
Bake the crust in the preheated oven for 20-25 minutes, or until it's lightly golden brown.
While the crust is baking, prepare the lemon filling. In a bowl, whisk together the granulated sugar and flour. Add the eggs, lemon juice, and lemon zest, and whisk until well combined.
Once the crust is baked, pour the lemon filling over the hot crust.
Reduce the oven temperature to 325°F (163°C) and bake for an additional 25-30 minutes, or until the lemon filling is set and the edges are lightly golden.

Allow the lemon bars to cool completely in the pan on a wire rack. Once cooled, refrigerate for at least 2 hours before cutting into squares.
Dust the tops with powdered sugar before serving, if desired.

These lemon bars are a perfect combination of sweet and tart, making them a refreshing treat for any occasion. Enjoy!

Cinnamon Rolls

Ingredients:

For the dough:

- 1 cup warm milk (about 110°F or 43°C)
- 2 1/4 teaspoons active dry yeast
- 1/4 cup granulated sugar
- 1/3 cup unsalted butter, melted
- 1 teaspoon salt
- 3 1/4 cups all-purpose flour
- 1 large egg

For the filling:

- 1/2 cup unsalted butter, softened
- 3/4 cup packed brown sugar
- 2 tablespoons ground cinnamon

For the cream cheese glaze:

- 4 ounces cream cheese, softened
- 1/4 cup unsalted butter, softened
- 1 cup powdered sugar
- 1/2 teaspoon vanilla extract

Instructions:

In a small bowl, combine the warm milk, active dry yeast, and a pinch of sugar. Let it sit for 5-10 minutes until it becomes frothy.
In a large bowl or the bowl of a stand mixer, combine the melted butter, sugar, and salt. Add the yeast mixture and mix well.
Gradually add the flour, one cup at a time, mixing well after each addition. Add the egg and continue to mix until a soft dough forms.
Knead the dough on a floured surface or in the stand mixer for about 5-7 minutes until it becomes smooth and elastic.
Place the dough in a greased bowl, cover it with a damp cloth, and let it rise in a warm place for about 1-2 hours or until it doubles in size.

Preheat your oven to 350°F (175°C). Roll out the dough on a floured surface into a rectangle, about 16x12 inches.

Spread the softened butter over the dough, leaving a small border around the edges. Sprinkle the brown sugar and cinnamon evenly over the butter.

Starting from one long edge, tightly roll the dough into a log. Cut the log into 12 even slices.

Place the slices in a greased baking pan, leaving a little space between each roll. Let them rise for an additional 20-30 minutes.

Bake in the preheated oven for 20-25 minutes or until the rolls are golden brown. While the rolls are baking, prepare the cream cheese glaze by beating together the cream cheese, butter, powdered sugar, and vanilla extract until smooth.

Once the cinnamon rolls are done baking, let them cool for a few minutes before drizzling the cream cheese glaze over the top.

Serve the cinnamon rolls warm and enjoy this delightful, gooey treat!

Apple Pie

Ingredients:

For the pie crust:

- 2 1/2 cups all-purpose flour
- 1 cup unsalted butter, chilled and cubed
- 1 teaspoon salt
- 1 tablespoon granulated sugar
- 1/4 to 1/2 cup ice water

For the apple filling:

- 6-7 cups peeled, cored, and thinly sliced apples (such as Granny Smith or a mix of varieties)
- 3/4 cup granulated sugar
- 1/4 cup brown sugar
- 1 tablespoon lemon juice
- 1 teaspoon ground cinnamon
- 1/4 teaspoon ground nutmeg
- 2 tablespoons all-purpose flour
- 1 tablespoon unsalted butter, cut into small pieces

For assembling:

- 1 egg (for egg wash)
- 1 tablespoon milk or cream (for egg wash)
- Additional granulated sugar (for sprinkling on top)

Instructions:

1. Prepare the Pie Crust:

- In a food processor, combine the flour, salt, and sugar. Add the chilled butter cubes and pulse until the mixture resembles coarse crumbs.

- Slowly add the ice water, 1 tablespoon at a time, and pulse until the dough comes together. Be careful not to overmix.
- Divide the dough in half, shape each half into a disk, wrap in plastic wrap, and refrigerate for at least 1 hour.

2. Preheat the Oven:

- Preheat your oven to 375°F (190°C).

3. Prepare the Apple Filling:

- In a large bowl, combine the sliced apples, granulated sugar, brown sugar, lemon juice, cinnamon, nutmeg, and flour. Toss until the apples are evenly coated.

4. Roll Out the Pie Crust:

- On a floured surface, roll out one disk of the chilled pie dough to fit a 9-inch pie dish. Place the rolled-out dough in the pie dish.

5. Fill the Pie:

- Spoon the apple filling into the prepared pie crust. Dot the top with small pieces of butter.

6. Roll Out the Top Crust:

- Roll out the second disk of pie dough and place it over the apples. Trim any excess dough, leaving a small overhang.

7. Seal and Decorate:

- Press the edges of the top and bottom crusts together to seal the pie. Crimp the edges with a fork or your fingers. Cut a few slits in the top crust to allow steam to escape.

8. Brush with Egg Wash:

- In a small bowl, whisk together the egg and milk or cream to create an egg wash. Brush the top crust with the egg wash, and sprinkle with additional granulated sugar.

9. Bake:

- Place the pie on a baking sheet to catch any drips and bake in the preheated oven for about 50-60 minutes, or until the crust is golden brown and the filling is bubbly.

10. Cool and Serve:

- Allow the pie to cool for at least 2 hours before serving. Serve slices with a scoop of vanilla ice cream if desired.

Enjoy your homemade apple pie!

Raspberry Almond Scones

Ingredients:

For the scones:

- 2 cups all-purpose flour
- 1/3 cup granulated sugar
- 1 tablespoon baking powder
- 1/2 teaspoon salt
- 1/2 cup unsalted butter, cold and cut into small pieces
- 1/2 cup sliced almonds
- 1/2 cup fresh or frozen raspberries
- 3/4 cup heavy cream
- 1 teaspoon almond extract
- Zest of one lemon

For the glaze:

- 1 cup powdered sugar
- 2 tablespoons milk or cream
- 1/2 teaspoon almond extract
- Sliced almonds (for garnish, optional)

Instructions:

1. Preheat the Oven:

- Preheat your oven to 400°F (200°C). Line a baking sheet with parchment paper.

2. Prepare the Scone Dough:

- In a large bowl, whisk together the flour, sugar, baking powder, and salt.
- Add the cold, cubed butter to the dry ingredients. Use a pastry cutter or your fingertips to work the butter into the flour until the mixture resembles coarse crumbs.
- Gently fold in the sliced almonds, raspberries, and lemon zest.

3. Combine Wet Ingredients:

   - In a separate bowl, mix together the heavy cream and almond extract.

4. Form the Dough:

   - Make a well in the center of the dry ingredients and pour in the cream mixture. Stir until just combined. Do not overmix.

5. Shape and Cut:

   - Turn the dough out onto a floured surface and gently knead it a few times. Pat the dough into a circle about 1 inch thick. Cut the circle into 8 wedges.

6. Bake:

   - Place the scones on the prepared baking sheet, leaving some space between each one. Bake in the preheated oven for 15-18 minutes, or until the scones are golden brown.

7. Prepare the Glaze:

   - While the scones are baking, prepare the glaze. In a bowl, whisk together the powdered sugar, milk or cream, and almond extract until smooth.

8. Glaze the Scones:

   - Once the scones have cooled for a few minutes, drizzle the glaze over the top. Optionally, garnish with sliced almonds.

9. Serve:

   - Allow the glaze to set for a few minutes before serving. Serve the scones warm and enjoy!

These raspberry almond scones are best enjoyed fresh out of the oven, and they pair wonderfully with a cup of tea or coffee.

Chocolate Lava Cake

Ingredients:

- 1/2 cup (1 stick) unsalted butter
- 4 ounces (about 2/3 cup) high-quality dark chocolate, chopped
- 1 cup powdered sugar
- 2 large eggs
- 2 large egg yolks
- 1 teaspoon vanilla extract
- 1/4 cup all-purpose flour
- Pinch of salt
- Optional: Additional butter and cocoa powder for greasing and dusting the ramekins

Instructions:

1. Preheat the Oven:

- Preheat your oven to 425°F (220°C). Grease the bottoms and sides of four 6-ounce ramekins with butter and dust with cocoa powder. This will help the cakes release easily.

2. Melt Chocolate and Butter:

- In a heatproof bowl set over a pan of simmering water (double boiler), melt the butter and chopped chocolate, stirring until smooth. Alternatively, you can melt them in the microwave, stirring every 20-30 seconds until smooth. Remove from heat and let it cool slightly.

3. Prepare Batter:

- In a separate bowl, whisk together the powdered sugar, eggs, egg yolks, and vanilla extract until well combined.

4. Combine Mixtures:

- Pour the melted chocolate mixture into the egg mixture and whisk until well combined.

5. Add Flour and Salt:

    - Sift in the flour and add a pinch of salt. Gently fold the flour and salt into the chocolate mixture until just combined. Be careful not to overmix.

6. Fill Ramekins:

    - Divide the batter equally among the prepared ramekins.

7. Bake:

    - Place the filled ramekins on a baking sheet and bake in the preheated oven for about 12-15 minutes. The edges should be set, but the center should still be soft.

8. Serve:

    - Carefully run a knife around the edges of each cake to loosen it. Invert each ramekin onto a serving plate, tapping the bottom to release the cake. The center should be gooey and molten.

9. Garnish (Optional):

    - Dust with powdered sugar, cocoa powder, or a scoop of vanilla ice cream before serving.

Serve the chocolate lava cakes immediately while the center is still warm and gooey. They are a perfect treat for chocolate lovers and make an impressive dessert for special occasions. Enjoy!

Buttermilk Biscuits

Ingredients:

- 2 cups all-purpose flour
- 1 tablespoon baking powder
- 1/2 teaspoon baking soda
- 1/2 teaspoon salt
- 1/2 cup unsalted butter, cold and cut into small pieces
- 1 cup buttermilk, cold

Instructions:

1. Preheat the Oven:

- Preheat your oven to 450°F (230°C).

2. Prepare the Dry Ingredients:

- In a large mixing bowl, whisk together the all-purpose flour, baking powder, baking soda, and salt.

3. Add Cold Butter:

- Add the cold, cubed butter to the dry ingredients. Using a pastry cutter or your fingers, cut the butter into the flour mixture until it resembles coarse crumbs. The key is to keep the butter cold for flaky biscuits.

4. Incorporate Buttermilk:

- Make a well in the center of the mixture and pour in the cold buttermilk. Stir with a fork until the dough comes together. Be careful not to overmix; it's okay if there are a few lumps.

5. Knead the Dough:

- Turn the dough out onto a floured surface. Gently knead it a few times, just until it holds together. Pat or roll the dough to about 1/2 to 3/4 inch thick.

6. Cut Out Biscuits:

- Using a round biscuit cutter or the rim of a glass, cut out biscuits from the dough. Place the cut biscuits on an ungreased baking sheet, with the sides touching for soft edges or slightly apart for crisp edges.

7. Bake:

- Bake in the preheated oven for 10-12 minutes or until the biscuits are golden brown on top.

8. Serve Warm:

- Serve the buttermilk biscuits warm, either on their own, with butter, jam, or as a side for your favorite meals.

Enjoy these homemade buttermilk biscuits as a delightful addition to your breakfast or as a side to your favorite dishes!

Key Lime Pie

Ingredients:

For the crust:

- 1 1/2 cups graham cracker crumbs
- 1/3 cup granulated sugar
- 6 tablespoons unsalted butter, melted

For the filling:

- 3 cups sweetened condensed milk
- 1/2 cup sour cream
- 3/4 cup key lime juice (freshly squeezed if possible)
- Zest of 2 limes
- 4 large egg yolks

For the whipped cream topping:

- 1 cup heavy cream
- 2 tablespoons powdered sugar
- 1/2 teaspoon vanilla extract

Instructions:

1. Preheat the Oven:

- Preheat your oven to 350°F (175°C).

2. Make the Graham Cracker Crust:

- In a medium bowl, combine the graham cracker crumbs, sugar, and melted butter. Press the mixture firmly into the bottom and up the sides of a 9-inch pie dish to form the crust.

3. Bake the Crust:

- Bake the crust in the preheated oven for 8-10 minutes or until it's set and lightly golden. Allow it to cool while you prepare the filling.

4. Prepare the Filling:

- In a large bowl, whisk together the sweetened condensed milk, sour cream, key lime juice, lime zest, and egg yolks until well combined.

5. Pour into Crust:

- Pour the filling into the prepared graham cracker crust, spreading it evenly.

6. Bake the Pie:

- Bake the pie in the preheated oven for 15-20 minutes or until the filling is set. It should still have a slight jiggle in the center.

7. Chill the Pie:

- Allow the Key Lime Pie to cool to room temperature, then refrigerate it for at least 4 hours or overnight to set completely.

8. Make the Whipped Cream:

- In a chilled bowl, whip the heavy cream, powdered sugar, and vanilla extract until stiff peaks form.

9. Serve:

- Once the pie is fully chilled, top it with the whipped cream. You can garnish with additional lime zest or slices if desired.

10. Enjoy:

- Slice and serve the Key Lime Pie chilled. It's a delightful and tangy treat, perfect for warm weather or any occasion.

This recipe captures the essence of the classic Key Lime Pie, delivering a perfect balance of sweetness and tartness. Enjoy!

Carrot Cake with Cream Cheese Frosting

Ingredients:

For the carrot cake:

- 2 cups all-purpose flour
- 2 cups grated carrots (about 3-4 medium carrots)
- 1 cup granulated sugar
- 1 cup packed brown sugar
- 1 cup vegetable oil
- 4 large eggs
- 1 teaspoon vanilla extract
- 1 teaspoon baking powder
- 1/2 teaspoon baking soda
- 1/2 teaspoon salt
- 1 teaspoon ground cinnamon
- 1/2 teaspoon ground nutmeg (optional)
- 1/2 cup crushed pineapple, drained (optional)
- 1/2 cup chopped walnuts or pecans (optional)

For the cream cheese frosting:

- 8 ounces cream cheese, softened
- 1/2 cup unsalted butter, softened
- 4 cups powdered sugar
- 1 teaspoon vanilla extract

Instructions:

1. Preheat the Oven:

    - Preheat your oven to 350°F (175°C). Grease and flour two 9-inch round cake pans.

2. Prepare the Carrot Cake Batter:

- In a large mixing bowl, whisk together the flour, baking powder, baking soda, salt, cinnamon, and nutmeg (if using).
- In another bowl, combine the grated carrots, granulated sugar, brown sugar, oil, eggs, and vanilla extract. Mix until well combined.
- Add the wet ingredients to the dry ingredients and stir until just combined. Fold in the crushed pineapple and chopped nuts if using.

3. Bake the Cake:

- Divide the batter evenly between the prepared cake pans. Bake in the preheated oven for 25-30 minutes or until a toothpick inserted into the center comes out clean.

4. Cool the Cake:

- Allow the cakes to cool in the pans for 10 minutes, then transfer them to a wire rack to cool completely.

5. Prepare the Cream Cheese Frosting:

- In a large bowl, beat together the softened cream cheese and butter until smooth and creamy. Add the powdered sugar and vanilla extract, and continue to beat until well combined.

6. Frost the Cake:

- Once the cakes are completely cooled, spread a layer of cream cheese frosting on top of one cake layer. Place the second cake layer on top and frost the top and sides of the entire cake.

7. Optional: Decorate and Garnish:

- Optionally, decorate the cake with additional chopped nuts or grated carrots.

8. Chill (Optional):

- For best results, refrigerate the carrot cake for at least 1-2 hours before serving to allow the frosting to set.

9. Slice and Serve:

- Slice and serve the carrot cake, enjoying the perfect combination of moist cake and creamy frosting.

This carrot cake is a crowd-pleaser and a great choice for special occasions or as a comforting dessert. Enjoy!

Pecan Pie Bars

Ingredients:

For the crust:

- 1 1/2 cups all-purpose flour
- 1/2 cup unsalted butter, softened
- 1/4 cup granulated sugar
- 1/4 teaspoon salt

For the pecan filling:

- 1 cup light corn syrup
- 1 cup packed light brown sugar
- 1/4 cup unsalted butter, melted
- 3 large eggs
- 1 teaspoon vanilla extract
- 2 cups chopped pecans

Instructions:

1. Preheat the Oven:

- Preheat your oven to 350°F (175°C). Grease a 9x13-inch baking dish.

2. Make the Crust:

- In a bowl, combine the flour, softened butter, sugar, and salt. Mix until crumbly. Press the mixture into the bottom of the prepared baking dish to form an even crust.

3. Bake the Crust:

- Bake the crust in the preheated oven for 15-20 minutes or until lightly golden. Remove it from the oven and set aside.

4. Prepare the Pecan Filling:

- In a mixing bowl, whisk together the corn syrup, brown sugar, melted butter, eggs, and vanilla extract until well combined. Stir in the chopped pecans.

5. Pour Over the Crust:

- Pour the pecan filling over the pre-baked crust, spreading it evenly.

6. Bake Again:

- Return the baking dish to the oven and bake for an additional 25-30 minutes or until the filling is set. A toothpick inserted into the center should come out with a few moist crumbs.

7. Cool and Slice:

- Allow the pecan pie bars to cool completely in the baking dish on a wire rack. Once cooled, refrigerate for at least 2 hours before slicing.

8. Slice and Serve:

- Slice the chilled pecan pie bars into squares or rectangles. Serve and enjoy!

These pecan pie bars offer all the deliciousness of pecan pie in a portable and easy-to-share form. They are perfect for holiday gatherings or any time you crave the rich, nutty flavor of pecans.

Italian Cannoli

Ingredients:

For the Cannoli Shells:

- 2 cups all-purpose flour
- 2 tablespoons granulated sugar
- 1/4 teaspoon salt
- 2 tablespoons unsalted butter, cold and cut into small pieces
- 1/2 cup dry white wine
- 1 large egg white (for sealing)

For the Ricotta Filling:

- 2 cups whole milk ricotta cheese, drained
- 1 cup powdered sugar
- 1 teaspoon vanilla extract
- 1/2 cup mini chocolate chips
- Optional: Chopped pistachios, candied orange peel for garnish

Instructions:

1. Make the Cannoli Shells:

- In a large bowl, whisk together the flour, sugar, and salt. Add the cold butter pieces and use your fingers to rub the butter into the flour until it resembles coarse crumbs.
- Gradually add the white wine and mix until the dough comes together. Knead the dough on a floured surface until it becomes smooth.
- Wrap the dough in plastic wrap and let it rest at room temperature for at least 30 minutes.
- Roll out the dough on a floured surface to about 1/8 inch thickness. Use a round cookie cutter to cut circles from the dough.
- Wrap each circle around a cannoli tube or form, sealing the edge with a little egg white.

- Heat oil in a deep fryer or a large pot to 350°F (175°C). Fry the cannoli shells until golden brown, then remove and let them cool before carefully removing the tubes.

2. Prepare the Ricotta Filling:

- In a medium bowl, mix together the drained ricotta, powdered sugar, and vanilla extract until smooth and creamy.
- Fold in the mini chocolate chips. Optionally, add chopped pistachios or candied orange peel for extra flavor and texture.
- Refrigerate the ricotta filling for at least 1 hour to allow it to set.

3. Fill the Cannoli:

- Fill a pastry bag with the ricotta filling and pipe it into both ends of each cannoli shell.
- Optionally, dip the ends of the filled cannoli in chopped pistachios or grated chocolate for a decorative touch.

4. Serve:

- Serve the cannoli immediately to maintain the crispiness of the shells. Dust with powdered sugar before serving if desired.

Enjoy these homemade Italian Cannoli as a delightful and authentic dessert! They are perfect for special occasions or whenever you crave a taste of Italy.

Banana Bread

Ingredients:

- 3 ripe bananas, mashed
- 2 large eggs
- 1 cup granulated sugar
- 1/4 cup unsalted butter, melted
- 1 teaspoon vanilla extract
- 1 1/2 cups all-purpose flour
- 1 teaspoon baking soda
- 1/2 teaspoon salt
- 1/2 teaspoon ground cinnamon (optional)
- 1/2 cup chopped nuts or chocolate chips (optional)

Instructions:

1. Preheat the Oven:

- Preheat your oven to 350°F (175°C). Grease a 9x5-inch loaf pan.

2. Mash the Bananas:

- In a large mixing bowl, mash the ripe bananas with a fork or potato masher until smooth.

3. Mix Wet Ingredients:

- Add the eggs, granulated sugar, melted butter, and vanilla extract to the mashed bananas. Mix well until the ingredients are combined.

4. Combine Dry Ingredients:

- In a separate bowl, whisk together the flour, baking soda, salt, and ground cinnamon if using.

5. Mix Wet and Dry Ingredients:

- Add the dry ingredients to the banana mixture and stir until just combined. Be careful not to overmix; a few lumps are okay.

6. Add Optional Ingredients:

- Fold in the chopped nuts or chocolate chips if desired.

7. Pour into Pan:

- Pour the batter into the greased loaf pan, spreading it evenly.

8. Bake:

- Bake in the preheated oven for 60-70 minutes or until a toothpick inserted into the center comes out clean or with a few moist crumbs.

9. Cool:

- Allow the banana bread to cool in the pan for about 10 minutes, then transfer it to a wire rack to cool completely.

10. Slice and Serve:

- Once cooled, slice the banana bread and serve. It's delicious on its own or with a spread of butter.

Enjoy your homemade banana bread! It's a great way to use up ripe bananas and makes for a tasty breakfast or snack.

Flourless Chocolate Cake

Ingredients:

- 1 cup (2 sticks) unsalted butter
- 1 1/4 cups granulated sugar
- 1 cup unsweetened cocoa powder
- 1 teaspoon instant coffee or espresso powder (optional, enhances chocolate flavor)
- 1/4 teaspoon salt
- 1 teaspoon vanilla extract
- 4 large eggs
- 1 cup semisweet or bittersweet chocolate chips (optional, for extra richness)

Instructions:

1. Preheat the Oven:

- Preheat your oven to 375°F (190°C). Grease a 9-inch round cake pan and line the bottom with parchment paper.

2. Melt Butter and Cocoa:

- In a medium saucepan over low heat, melt the butter. Once melted, add the granulated sugar, cocoa powder, instant coffee (if using), and salt. Stir until well combined. Remove from heat.

3. Add Vanilla Extract:

- Stir in the vanilla extract and let the mixture cool slightly.

4. Add Eggs:

- Add the eggs one at a time, mixing well after each addition. The batter should become smooth and glossy.

5. Fold in Chocolate Chips (Optional):

- If using chocolate chips, fold them into the batter until evenly distributed.

6. Pour into Pan:

   - Pour the batter into the prepared cake pan and smooth the top with a spatula.

7. Bake:

   - Bake in the preheated oven for about 25-30 minutes or until the cake has set and a toothpick inserted into the center comes out with moist crumbs (not wet batter).

8. Cool:

   - Allow the cake to cool in the pan for about 10-15 minutes. Then, run a knife around the edge of the pan and invert the cake onto a serving plate. Remove the parchment paper.

9. Optional: Dust with Cocoa Powder:

   - Dust the top of the cake with cocoa powder for a finishing touch.

10. Serve:

    - Slice and serve the flourless chocolate cake. It's delicious on its own or with a dollop of whipped cream or a scoop of vanilla ice cream.

This flourless chocolate cake is dense, fudgy, and intensely chocolatey. It's a perfect dessert for special occasions or when you're craving a luxurious chocolate treat. Enjoy!

Pumpkin Spice Latte Cupcakes

Ingredients:

For the cupcakes:

- 1 3/4 cups all-purpose flour
- 1 teaspoon baking powder
- 1/2 teaspoon baking soda
- 1/2 teaspoon salt
- 1 1/2 teaspoons ground cinnamon
- 1 teaspoon ground ginger
- 1/2 teaspoon ground nutmeg
- 1/4 teaspoon ground cloves
- 1/2 cup unsalted butter, softened
- 1 cup granulated sugar
- 1/2 cup packed brown sugar
- 2 large eggs
- 1 cup canned pumpkin puree
- 1/2 cup strong brewed coffee or espresso, cooled
- 1/4 cup milk
- 1 teaspoon vanilla extract

For the frosting:

- 8 ounces cream cheese, softened
- 1/2 cup unsalted butter, softened
- 4 cups powdered sugar
- 1 teaspoon vanilla extract
- 1/2 teaspoon ground cinnamon
- Optional: Whipped cream and cinnamon for garnish

Instructions:

1. Preheat the Oven:

- Preheat your oven to 350°F (175°C). Line a muffin tin with cupcake liners.

2. Make the Cupcake Batter:

- In a medium bowl, whisk together the flour, baking powder, baking soda, salt, cinnamon, ginger, nutmeg, and cloves.
- In a large bowl, cream together the softened butter, granulated sugar, and brown sugar until light and fluffy.
- Add the eggs one at a time, beating well after each addition. Stir in the pumpkin puree.
- In a small bowl, combine the brewed coffee or espresso, milk, and vanilla extract.
- Add the dry ingredients to the wet ingredients in three additions, alternating with the coffee mixture. Begin and end with the dry ingredients, mixing until just combined.

3. Fill the Cupcake Liners:

- Divide the batter evenly among the cupcake liners, filling each about two-thirds full.

4. Bake:

- Bake in the preheated oven for 18-20 minutes or until a toothpick inserted into the center comes out clean. Allow the cupcakes to cool in the tin for a few minutes before transferring them to a wire rack to cool completely.

5. Make the Cream Cheese Frosting:

- In a large bowl, beat together the softened cream cheese and butter until smooth and creamy.
- Add the powdered sugar, vanilla extract, and ground cinnamon. Beat until well combined.

6. Frost the Cupcakes:

- Once the cupcakes are completely cooled, frost them with the cream cheese frosting using a piping bag or a spatula.

7. Garnish (Optional):

- Optionally, garnish the cupcakes with a dollop of whipped cream and a sprinkle of ground cinnamon.

Enjoy these Pumpkin Spice Latte Cupcakes, a perfect fall-inspired treat that combines the flavors of pumpkin, spices, and a hint of coffee!

Almond Croissants

Ingredients:

For the croissants:

- 1 sheet of puff pastry (store-bought or homemade)
- 1/2 cup (1 stick) unsalted butter, cold but pliable
- Flour for dusting

For the almond filling:

- 1 cup almond flour
- 1/2 cup granulated sugar
- 1/2 cup unsalted butter, softened
- 1 large egg
- 1 teaspoon almond extract
- Sliced almonds for topping
- Powdered sugar for dusting (optional)

Instructions:

1. Prepare the Almond Filling:

- In a bowl, combine almond flour, granulated sugar, softened butter, egg, and almond extract. Mix until well combined. Set aside.

2. Roll Out the Puff Pastry:

- If using store-bought puff pastry, roll it out on a floured surface to a rectangle. If using homemade, roll it out to a similar size.

3. Add Butter Layer:

- Place the cold, pliable butter in the center of the puff pastry and fold the pastry over it like an envelope. Roll out the dough again into a rectangle.

4. Create Layers:

   - Fold the rectangle into thirds like a letter, creating layers. This process is known as laminating the dough. Chill the dough for about 30 minutes in the refrigerator.

5. Roll Out and Fold:

   - Repeat the rolling and folding process two more times, chilling the dough between each fold.

6. Cut and Shape:

   - Roll out the laminated dough into a large rectangle. Cut it into smaller rectangles or triangles, depending on your preference.

7. Add Almond Filling:

   - Spoon a generous amount of almond filling onto each piece of dough. Spread it out evenly.

8. Roll and Shape:

   - Roll up each piece of dough, starting from the wider end if you've cut triangles. Place the shaped almond croissants on a baking sheet lined with parchment paper, seam side down.

9. Proof:

   - Allow the shaped croissants to proof for about 1-2 hours or until they have doubled in size.

10. Preheat the Oven:

    - Preheat your oven to 375°F (190°C).

11. Bake:

- Brush the tops of the almond croissants with a beaten egg and sprinkle sliced almonds on top. Bake in the preheated oven for 15-20 minutes or until golden brown.

12. Optional: Dust with Powdered Sugar:

- If desired, dust the almond croissants with powdered sugar after they come out of the oven.

13. Cool:

- Allow the almond croissants to cool slightly before serving. They can be enjoyed warm or at room temperature.

Enjoy these homemade almond croissants with a cup of coffee for a delightful breakfast or snack!

Tiramisu

Ingredients:

- 6 large egg yolks
- 1 cup granulated sugar
- 1 1/4 cups mascarpone cheese, softened
- 1 1/2 cups heavy cream
- 1 cup strong brewed coffee or espresso, cooled
- 1/4 cup coffee liqueur (optional)
- 24-30 ladyfinger cookies (savoiardi)
- Cocoa powder, for dusting

Instructions:

1. Prepare the Coffee Mixture:

- Brew strong coffee or espresso and let it cool. If using espresso, you may sweeten it with sugar to taste. Add the coffee liqueur to the cooled coffee, if desired.

2. Make the Mascarpone Mixture:

- In a large bowl, whisk together the egg yolks and granulated sugar until the mixture is pale and slightly thickened.
- Add the softened mascarpone cheese to the egg yolk mixture and beat until smooth and well combined.

3. Whip the Heavy Cream:

- In a separate bowl, whip the heavy cream until stiff peaks form.

4. Combine the Mixtures:

- Gently fold the whipped cream into the mascarpone mixture until smooth and well incorporated. Be careful not to deflate the whipped cream.

5. Assemble the Tiramisu:

- Dip each ladyfinger into the coffee mixture for a couple of seconds, ensuring they are soaked but not overly saturated.
- Arrange a layer of dipped ladyfingers in the bottom of a serving dish or individual glasses.
- Spoon a layer of the mascarpone mixture over the ladyfingers, spreading it evenly.
- Repeat the layers until you run out of ingredients, finishing with a layer of the mascarpone mixture on top.

6. Refrigerate:

- Cover the tiramisu with plastic wrap and refrigerate for at least 4 hours or preferably overnight. This allows the flavors to meld and the dessert to set.

7. Dust with Cocoa Powder:

- Before serving, dust the top of the tiramisu with cocoa powder using a fine-mesh sieve or sifter.

8. Serve:

- Slice or scoop servings, and enjoy this creamy and indulgent Italian dessert!

Tiramisu is a wonderful make-ahead dessert and is perfect for special occasions or any time you're craving a delightful and sophisticated treat.

Chocolate Eclairs

Ingredients:

For the Choux Pastry:

- 1 cup water
- 1/2 cup unsalted butter
- 1 cup all-purpose flour
- 4 large eggs

For the Pastry Cream Filling:

- 2 cups whole milk
- 4 large egg yolks
- 1/2 cup granulated sugar
- 1/4 cup cornstarch
- 1 teaspoon vanilla extract

For the Chocolate Glaze:

- 4 ounces semisweet or bittersweet chocolate, chopped
- 1/2 cup heavy cream
- 2 tablespoons unsalted butter
- 2 tablespoons corn syrup (optional, for shine)

Instructions:

1. Make the Choux Pastry:

- Preheat your oven to 425°F (220°C). Line a baking sheet with parchment paper.
- In a saucepan, combine water and butter. Bring to a boil, then remove from heat. Stir in the flour until the mixture forms a ball.
- Transfer the dough to a mixing bowl. Using a hand mixer or a stand mixer, beat in the eggs one at a time, ensuring each egg is fully incorporated before adding the next.

- Place the dough in a pastry bag fitted with a large round tip. Pipe 4-inch-long lines onto the prepared baking sheet, leaving space between each eclair.
- Bake in the preheated oven for 15-20 minutes or until the eclairs are puffed and golden brown. Reduce the oven temperature to 375°F (190°C) and continue baking for an additional 10-15 minutes. Allow the eclairs to cool completely.

2. Prepare the Pastry Cream Filling:

- In a saucepan, heat the milk until it just starts to simmer.
- In a bowl, whisk together the egg yolks, sugar, and cornstarch until well combined. Slowly pour the hot milk into the egg mixture, whisking constantly.
- Return the mixture to the saucepan and cook over medium heat, stirring constantly, until it thickens. Remove from heat, stir in the vanilla extract, and let it cool.

3. Fill the Eclairs:

- Once the eclairs are completely cooled, cut them in half horizontally. Pipe or spoon the pastry cream into the bottom half of each eclair.

4. Make the Chocolate Glaze:

- In a heatproof bowl, combine the chopped chocolate, heavy cream, butter, and corn syrup. Heat the mixture over a double boiler or in the microwave, stirring until smooth.

5. Glaze the Eclairs:

- Dip the top of each filled eclair into the chocolate glaze, allowing any excess to drip off. Place the glazed eclairs on a serving platter.

6. Chill:

- Place the chocolate eclairs in the refrigerator for at least 30 minutes to allow the glaze to set.

7. Serve:

- Once the chocolate glaze has set, serve the chocolate eclairs and enjoy these delicious pastries!

Chocolate eclairs are a delightful treat, perfect for special occasions or as a decadent dessert. Enjoy making and savoring these classic French pastries!

Maple Pecan Cinnamon Rolls

Ingredients:

For the Dough:

- 1 cup warm milk (about 110°F or 43°C)
- 2 1/4 teaspoons (1 packet) active dry yeast
- 1/4 cup granulated sugar
- 1/3 cup unsalted butter, melted
- 1 teaspoon salt
- 3 1/4 cups all-purpose flour
- 1 large egg

For the Filling:

- 1/2 cup unsalted butter, softened
- 1 cup brown sugar, packed
- 2 tablespoons ground cinnamon

For the Maple Pecan Topping:

- 1/2 cup unsalted butter
- 1 cup pecans, chopped
- 1/2 cup maple syrup

Instructions:

1. Activate the Yeast:

- In a bowl, combine warm milk, sugar, and active dry yeast. Let it sit for about 5-10 minutes until the mixture becomes frothy.

2. Make the Dough:

- In a large mixing bowl, combine the activated yeast mixture, melted butter, salt, egg, and flour. Mix until the dough comes together.
- Knead the dough on a floured surface for about 5-7 minutes until it becomes smooth and elastic.

- Place the dough in a greased bowl, cover it with a clean kitchen towel, and let it rise in a warm place for about 1-1.5 hours or until it doubles in size.

3. Roll Out the Dough:

- Preheat your oven to 350°F (175°C). Roll out the risen dough on a floured surface into a large rectangle.

4. Prepare the Filling:

- Spread the softened butter over the rolled-out dough. In a bowl, mix together brown sugar and ground cinnamon. Sprinkle this mixture evenly over the butter.

5. Roll and Cut:

- Starting from one of the longer sides, roll the dough into a log. Slice the log into equal-sized cinnamon rolls.

6. Make the Maple Pecan Topping:

- In a saucepan, melt the butter for the topping. Stir in the chopped pecans and maple syrup.

7. Assemble and Bake:

- Pour the maple pecan mixture into the bottom of a greased baking dish. Place the cinnamon rolls on top of the maple pecan mixture.
- Bake in the preheated oven for about 25-30 minutes or until the cinnamon rolls are golden brown and cooked through.

8. Cool and Serve:

- Allow the maple pecan cinnamon rolls to cool for a few minutes before serving. You can invert the rolls onto a serving plate so that the maple pecan topping is on top.

These maple pecan cinnamon rolls are a delicious treat for breakfast or brunch, and the combination of flavors adds a delightful twist to the classic cinnamon roll recipe. Enjoy!

Strawberry Shortcake

Ingredients:

For the Shortcakes:

- 2 cups all-purpose flour
- 1/4 cup granulated sugar
- 1 tablespoon baking powder
- 1/2 teaspoon salt
- 1/2 cup unsalted butter, cold and cut into small pieces
- 3/4 cup whole milk
- 1 teaspoon vanilla extract

For the Strawberries:

- 4 cups fresh strawberries, hulled and sliced
- 1/4 cup granulated sugar

For the Whipped Cream:

- 1 cup heavy cream
- 2 tablespoons powdered sugar
- 1 teaspoon vanilla extract

Instructions:

1. Preheat the Oven:

- Preheat your oven to 425°F (220°C). Line a baking sheet with parchment paper.

2. Make the Shortcakes:

- In a large mixing bowl, whisk together the flour, sugar, baking powder, and salt.
- Add the cold, diced butter to the dry ingredients. Use a pastry cutter or your fingers to cut the butter into the flour until it resembles coarse crumbs.

- Pour in the milk and vanilla extract. Stir until just combined; do not overmix.
- Turn the dough out onto a floured surface and gently knead it a few times. Pat or roll the dough to about 1/2 to 3/4 inch thick.
- Use a round biscuit cutter to cut out shortcakes. Place them on the prepared baking sheet.

3. Bake the Shortcakes:

- Bake in the preheated oven for 12-15 minutes or until the shortcakes are golden brown. Allow them to cool on a wire rack.

4. Prepare the Strawberries:

- In a bowl, combine the sliced strawberries and granulated sugar. Toss gently to coat the strawberries in sugar and let them macerate for about 15-30 minutes.

5. Make the Whipped Cream:

- In a chilled bowl, whip the heavy cream, powdered sugar, and vanilla extract until stiff peaks form.

6. Assemble the Strawberry Shortcakes:

- Once the shortcakes are cooled, split them in half horizontally.
- Spoon a generous amount of macerated strawberries onto the bottom half of each shortcake.
- Top with a dollop of whipped cream and place the other half of the shortcake on top.
- Optionally, garnish with additional whipped cream and a whole strawberry.

7. Serve:

- Serve the strawberry shortcakes immediately, and enjoy the delightful combination of buttery shortcakes, sweet strawberries, and whipped cream.

Strawberry shortcake is a classic summer dessert that is simple to make and always a crowd-pleaser. Enjoy this delicious treat during strawberry season or whenever you're in the mood for a light and fruity dessert!

Peanut Butter Blossom Cookies

Ingredients:

- 1/2 cup (1 stick) unsalted butter, softened
- 1/2 cup granulated sugar
- 1/2 cup packed light brown sugar
- 1/2 cup creamy peanut butter
- 1 large egg
- 1 teaspoon vanilla extract
- 1 3/4 cups all-purpose flour
- 1 teaspoon baking soda
- 1/2 teaspoon salt
- Additional granulated sugar for rolling
- About 36 Hershey's Kisses, unwrapped

Instructions:

1. Preheat the Oven:

- Preheat your oven to 350°F (175°C). Line baking sheets with parchment paper.

2. Cream Together Wet Ingredients:

- In a large bowl, cream together the softened butter, granulated sugar, brown sugar, and peanut butter until light and fluffy.

3. Add Egg and Vanilla:

- Beat in the egg and vanilla extract until well combined.

4. Combine Dry Ingredients:

- In a separate bowl, whisk together the flour, baking soda, and salt.

5. Mix Wet and Dry Ingredients:

- Gradually add the dry ingredients to the wet ingredients, mixing until just combined. Avoid overmixing.

6. Shape and Roll:

- Shape the dough into 1-inch balls. Roll each ball in granulated sugar to coat.

7. Bake:

- Place the sugar-coated dough balls on the prepared baking sheets, spacing them about 2 inches apart.
- Bake in the preheated oven for 8-10 minutes or until the edges are lightly golden.

8. Add Hershey's Kisses:

- Remove the cookies from the oven and immediately press a Hershey's Kiss into the center of each cookie.

9. Cool:

- Allow the cookies to cool on the baking sheets for a few minutes before transferring them to wire racks to cool completely.

10. Serve:

- Once the cookies are completely cooled, serve and enjoy these classic Peanut Butter Blossom Cookies!

These cookies are a perfect combination of peanut butter and chocolate, making them a favorite for cookie lovers. They are often enjoyed during holidays and special occasions. Enjoy baking and indulging in these delightful treats!

Classic Eclairs

Ingredients:

For the Choux Pastry:

- 1 cup water
- 1/2 cup unsalted butter
- 1 cup all-purpose flour
- 4 large eggs

For the Vanilla Pastry Cream:

- 2 cups whole milk
- 1/2 cup granulated sugar
- 1/4 cup cornstarch
- 1/4 teaspoon salt
- 4 large egg yolks
- 2 tablespoons unsalted butter
- 1 teaspoon vanilla extract

For the Chocolate Glaze:

- 1/2 cup semisweet or bittersweet chocolate, chopped
- 1/2 cup heavy cream
- 2 tablespoons unsalted butter
- 2 tablespoons corn syrup (optional, for shine)

Instructions:

1. Make the Choux Pastry:

- Preheat your oven to 425°F (220°C). Line a baking sheet with parchment paper.
- In a saucepan, combine water and butter. Bring to a boil, then remove from heat. Stir in the flour until the mixture forms a ball.

- Transfer the dough to a mixing bowl. Using a hand mixer or a stand mixer, beat in the eggs one at a time, ensuring each egg is fully incorporated before adding the next.
- Place the dough in a pastry bag fitted with a large round tip. Pipe 4-inch-long lines onto the prepared baking sheet, leaving space between each eclair.
- Bake in the preheated oven for 15-20 minutes or until the eclairs are puffed and golden brown. Allow them to cool on a wire rack.

2. Make the Vanilla Pastry Cream:

- In a saucepan, heat the milk until it just starts to simmer.
- In a bowl, whisk together sugar, cornstarch, salt, and egg yolks until well combined. Slowly pour the hot milk into the egg mixture, whisking constantly.
- Return the mixture to the saucepan and cook over medium heat, stirring constantly, until it thickens. Remove from heat, stir in butter and vanilla extract, and let it cool.

3. Fill the Eclairs:

- Once the eclairs are completely cooled, cut them in half horizontally. Pipe or spoon the pastry cream into the bottom half of each eclair.

4. Make the Chocolate Glaze:

- In a heatproof bowl, combine the chopped chocolate, heavy cream, butter, and corn syrup. Heat the mixture over a double boiler or in the microwave, stirring until smooth.

5. Glaze the Eclairs:

- Dip the top of each filled eclair into the chocolate glaze, allowing any excess to drip off. Place the glazed eclairs on a serving platter.

6. Chill:

- Place the chocolate eclairs in the refrigerator for at least 30 minutes to allow the glaze to set.

7. Serve:

- Once the chocolate glaze has set, serve the classic eclairs and enjoy!

These classic eclairs are a delightful and elegant dessert, perfect for special occasions or when you want to impress with your baking skills. Enjoy the combination of light pastry, creamy filling, and rich chocolate glaze!

Chocolate Babka

Ingredients:

For the Dough:

- 4 cups all-purpose flour
- 1/2 cup granulated sugar
- 1 packet (2 1/4 teaspoons) active dry yeast
- 1/2 teaspoon salt
- 1 cup whole milk, warmed
- 1/2 cup unsalted butter, softened
- 2 large eggs

For the Chocolate Filling:

- 1 cup semisweet chocolate, finely chopped
- 1/2 cup unsalted butter, melted
- 1/2 cup granulated sugar
- 1/4 cup unsweetened cocoa powder
- 1 teaspoon ground cinnamon (optional)

For the Syrup (optional):

- 1/2 cup water
- 1/2 cup granulated sugar

Instructions:

1. Make the Dough:

- In a bowl, combine warm milk and sugar. Sprinkle the yeast over the mixture and let it sit for about 5-10 minutes until it becomes frothy.
- In a large mixing bowl, combine the flour and salt. Add the softened butter, eggs, and the yeast mixture. Mix until a dough forms.
- Knead the dough on a floured surface for about 5-7 minutes until it becomes smooth and elastic. Place the dough in a greased bowl, cover it with a clean kitchen towel, and let it rise in a warm place for about 1-1.5 hours or until it doubles in size.

2. Make the Chocolate Filling:

   - In a bowl, combine the finely chopped chocolate, melted butter, sugar, cocoa powder, and ground cinnamon (if using). Mix until well combined.

3. Roll Out the Dough:

   - Preheat your oven to 350°F (175°C). Roll out the risen dough on a floured surface into a large rectangle.

4. Add the Chocolate Filling:

   - Spread the chocolate filling evenly over the rolled-out dough, leaving a small border around the edges.

5. Roll the Dough:

   - Starting from one of the longer sides, tightly roll the dough into a log.

6. Cut and Twist:

   - Use a sharp knife to cut the log in half lengthwise. Twist the two halves around each other, creating a twisted log.

7. Place in Pan:

   - Place the twisted dough into a greased loaf pan, ensuring the twisted layers are facing upwards.

8. Bake:

   - Bake in the preheated oven for about 30-35 minutes or until the babka is golden brown and cooked through. If the top is browning too quickly, you can cover it with foil during the last 10-15 minutes of baking.

9. Make the Syrup (Optional):

   - In a saucepan, combine water and sugar. Bring to a simmer, stirring until the sugar dissolves. Remove from heat.

10. Brush with Syrup (Optional):

    - Once the babka is out of the oven, brush the warm syrup over the top to add a shiny finish.

11. Cool:

    - Allow the chocolate babka to cool in the pan for about 15-20 minutes before transferring it to a wire rack to cool completely.

12. Slice and Serve:

    - Once cooled, slice and serve the Chocolate Babka. Enjoy the layers of chocolatey goodness!

Chocolate Babka is a beautiful and delicious pastry that's perfect for special occasions or whenever you want to indulge in a delightful sweet treat. Enjoy making and savoring this Eastern European classic!

Linzer Cookies

Ingredients:

For the Cookie Dough:

- 1 cup unsalted butter, softened
- 1/2 cup granulated sugar
- 1 cup ground almonds
- 1 teaspoon vanilla extract
- 1 egg
- 2 cups all-purpose flour
- 1/2 teaspoon baking powder
- 1/2 teaspoon ground cinnamon
- 1/4 teaspoon salt

For Filling and Dusting:

- Raspberry jam (or any preferred jam)
- Powdered sugar for dusting

Instructions:

1. Prepare the Dough:

- In a large bowl, cream together the softened butter and granulated sugar until light and fluffy.
- Add the ground almonds and vanilla extract, mixing until well combined.
- Beat in the egg until incorporated.
- In a separate bowl, whisk together the flour, baking powder, ground cinnamon, and salt.
- Gradually add the dry ingredients to the wet ingredients, mixing until a soft dough forms.

2. Chill the Dough:

- Divide the dough into two equal portions and shape each into a disk. Wrap them in plastic wrap and chill in the refrigerator for at least 1-2 hours or until firm.

3. Preheat the Oven:

- Preheat your oven to 350°F (175°C). Line baking sheets with parchment paper.

4. Roll Out the Dough:

- On a lightly floured surface, roll out one disk of dough to about 1/8-inch thickness.

5. Cut Out Shapes:

- Using a round cookie cutter, cut out an even number of circles. Then, use a smaller-shaped cutter to cut out the centers of half of the circles, creating a "window" effect.

6. Bake:

- Place the cookies on the prepared baking sheets and bake in the preheated oven for 10-12 minutes or until the edges are lightly golden.
- Allow the cookies to cool on the baking sheets for a few minutes before transferring them to wire racks to cool completely.

7. Assemble the Cookies:

- Spread a small amount of raspberry jam on the whole cookies (without the center cutout).
- Place the cutout cookies on top, creating a sandwich with the jam in the middle, allowing it to peek through the window.

8. Dust with Powdered Sugar:

- Dust the tops of the assembled Linzer cookies with powdered sugar.

9. Serve:

- Serve and enjoy these delightful and visually appealing Linzer cookies!

Linzer cookies are a wonderful addition to holiday cookie platters or any special occasion. The combination of buttery almond dough and sweet raspberry jam filling makes them a delightful treat for all to enjoy.

Almond Joy Brownies

Ingredients:

For the Brownie Base:

- 1 cup (2 sticks) unsalted butter
- 2 cups granulated sugar
- 4 large eggs
- 1 teaspoon vanilla extract
- 1 cup all-purpose flour
- 1/2 cup cocoa powder
- 1/2 teaspoon baking powder
- 1/4 teaspoon salt

For the Almond Joy Topping:

- 1 1/2 cups sweetened shredded coconut
- 1 cup sliced almonds
- 1 cup sweetened condensed milk
- 1 cup semisweet chocolate chips

Instructions:

1. Preheat the Oven:

- Preheat your oven to 350°F (175°C). Grease and line a 9x13-inch baking pan with parchment paper.

2. Make the Brownie Base:

- In a saucepan, melt the butter over low heat. Remove from heat and stir in the granulated sugar.
- Add the eggs one at a time, beating well after each addition. Stir in the vanilla extract.

- In a separate bowl, sift together the flour, cocoa powder, baking powder, and salt. Gradually add the dry ingredients to the wet ingredients, mixing until just combined.

3. Bake the Brownies:

- Pour the brownie batter into the prepared pan and spread it evenly.
- Bake in the preheated oven for 25-30 minutes or until a toothpick inserted into the center comes out with moist crumbs (not wet batter). Remove from the oven and let the brownies cool in the pan.

4. Prepare the Almond Joy Topping:

- In a bowl, mix together the shredded coconut, sliced almonds, and sweetened condensed milk until well combined.

5. Top the Brownies:

- Once the brownies are cooled, spread the coconut-almond mixture evenly over the top.

6. Melt the Chocolate:

- In a microwave-safe bowl or using a double boiler, melt the chocolate chips until smooth.

7. Drizzle the Chocolate:

- Drizzle the melted chocolate over the coconut-almond layer, creating a chocolate topping.

8. Chill:

- Place the brownies in the refrigerator for at least 1-2 hours to allow the chocolate to set.

9. Cut and Serve:

- Once fully chilled, use the parchment paper to lift the brownies out of the pan. Cut them into squares and serve.

Enjoy these Almond Joy brownies as a decadent and delightful treat, combining the classic flavors of chocolate, coconut, and almonds!

Lemon Poppy Seed Muffins

Ingredients:

- 2 cups all-purpose flour
- 1 cup granulated sugar
- 2 tablespoons poppy seeds
- 1 tablespoon baking powder
- 1/2 teaspoon baking soda
- 1/4 teaspoon salt
- 1 cup plain yogurt or Greek yogurt
- 1/2 cup unsalted butter, melted and cooled
- 2 large eggs
- 1 teaspoon vanilla extract
- Zest of 2 lemons
- 3 tablespoons fresh lemon juice

For the Lemon Glaze:

- 1 cup powdered sugar
- 2-3 tablespoons fresh lemon juice

Instructions:

1. Preheat the Oven:

- Preheat your oven to 375°F (190°C). Line a muffin tin with paper liners.

2. Mix Dry Ingredients:

- In a large bowl, whisk together the flour, sugar, poppy seeds, baking powder, baking soda, and salt.

3. Combine Wet Ingredients:

- In another bowl, mix together the yogurt, melted butter, eggs, vanilla extract, lemon zest, and lemon juice.

4. Combine Wet and Dry Ingredients:

- Pour the wet ingredients into the bowl with the dry ingredients. Stir until just combined. Do not overmix; a few lumps are okay.

5. Fill Muffin Cups:

- Spoon the batter into the prepared muffin cups, filling each about two-thirds full.

6. Bake:

- Bake in the preheated oven for 18-20 minutes or until a toothpick inserted into the center comes out clean or with a few moist crumbs.

7. Make Lemon Glaze:

- While the muffins are baking, prepare the lemon glaze. In a bowl, whisk together the powdered sugar and fresh lemon juice until smooth.

8. Glaze the Muffins:

- Once the muffins are done baking, allow them to cool in the muffin tin for a few minutes. Then, transfer them to a wire rack.
- Drizzle the lemon glaze over the warm muffins, allowing it to soak in.

9. Cool and Serve:

- Let the muffins cool completely before serving. Enjoy these lemon poppy seed muffins with a cup of tea or coffee!

These Lemon Poppy Seed Muffins are moist, flavorful, and have a burst of citrus goodness. The addition of poppy seeds adds a delightful crunch, and the lemon glaze provides a sweet and tangy finish. Perfect for brightening up your breakfast or snack time!

Black Forest Cake

Ingredients:

For the Chocolate Cake Layers:

- 2 cups all-purpose flour
- 2 cups granulated sugar
- 3/4 cup unsweetened cocoa powder
- 2 teaspoons baking powder
- 1/2 teaspoon baking soda
- 1/2 teaspoon salt
- 3 large eggs
- 1 cup whole milk
- 1/2 cup vegetable oil
- 2 teaspoons vanilla extract
- 1 cup boiling water

For the Filling and Topping:

- 2 cans (about 21 ounces total) of cherry pie filling
- 3 cups heavy cream
- 1/2 cup powdered sugar
- 1 teaspoon vanilla extract
- Chocolate shavings or grated chocolate for decoration

Instructions:

1. Preheat the Oven:

- Preheat your oven to 350°F (175°C). Grease and flour three 9-inch round cake pans.

2. Make the Chocolate Cake:

- In a large bowl, whisk together the flour, sugar, cocoa powder, baking powder, baking soda, and salt.

- Add the eggs, milk, oil, and vanilla extract. Mix until well combined.
- Gradually add the boiling water to the batter, mixing until smooth. The batter will be thin, but that's okay.
- Pour the batter evenly into the prepared cake pans.

3. Bake:

- Bake in the preheated oven for 30-35 minutes or until a toothpick inserted into the center of the cakes comes out clean.
- Allow the cakes to cool in the pans for 10 minutes, then transfer them to a wire rack to cool completely.

4. Whip the Cream:

- In a large mixing bowl, whip the heavy cream, powdered sugar, and vanilla extract until stiff peaks form.

5. Assemble the Cake:

- Place one cake layer on a serving plate. Spread a layer of whipped cream over the cake, followed by a layer of cherry pie filling.
- Repeat with the second cake layer, more whipped cream, and cherry pie filling.
- Place the third cake layer on top. Frost the top and sides of the cake with the remaining whipped cream.

6. Decorate:

- Decorate the top of the cake with additional cherry pie filling and chocolate shavings or grated chocolate.

7. Chill:

- Refrigerate the Black Forest Cake for at least 4 hours or overnight to allow the flavors to meld and the cake to set.

8. Serve:

- Slice and serve this delicious Black Forest Cake. Enjoy the combination of chocolate, whipped cream, and cherries!

This Black Forest Cake is a show-stopping dessert that's perfect for special occasions or celebrations. The layers of moist chocolate cake, fluffy whipped cream, and tart cherries create a delightful and indulgent treat.

Snickerdoodle Cookies

Ingredients:

For the Cookie Dough:

- 1 cup unsalted butter, softened
- 1 and 1/2 cups granulated sugar
- 2 large eggs
- 1 teaspoon vanilla extract
- 2 and 3/4 cups all-purpose flour
- 1 and 1/2 teaspoons cream of tartar
- 1/2 teaspoon baking soda
- 1/2 teaspoon salt

For the Cinnamon-Sugar Coating:

- 1/4 cup granulated sugar
- 1 tablespoon ground cinnamon

Instructions:

1. Preheat the Oven:

- Preheat your oven to 375°F (190°C). Line baking sheets with parchment paper.

2. Make the Cookie Dough:

- In a large bowl, cream together the softened butter and granulated sugar until light and fluffy.
- Add the eggs, one at a time, beating well after each addition. Stir in the vanilla extract.
- In a separate bowl, whisk together the flour, cream of tartar, baking soda, and salt.
- Gradually add the dry ingredients to the wet ingredients, mixing until just combined. Do not overmix.

3. Form Cookie Dough Balls:

- In a small bowl, mix together the sugar and ground cinnamon for the coating.

- Shape the cookie dough into 1-inch balls. Roll each ball in the cinnamon-sugar mixture, ensuring they are well coated.

4. Place on Baking Sheets:

- Place the coated cookie dough balls on the prepared baking sheets, spacing them about 2 inches apart.

5. Bake:

- Bake in the preheated oven for 8-10 minutes or until the edges are set and the centers are slightly soft.

6. Cool:

- Allow the cookies to cool on the baking sheets for a few minutes before transferring them to wire racks to cool completely.

7. Serve:

- Once cooled, serve and enjoy these classic Snickerdoodle cookies!

These Snickerdoodle cookies are sure to be a hit with their irresistible combination of cinnamon and sugar. They are perfect for any occasion and make a delicious treat for cookie lovers. Enjoy!

Coconut Cream Pie

Ingredients:

For the Pie Crust:

- 1 1/4 cups all-purpose flour
- 1/2 cup unsalted butter, cold and cut into small cubes
- 1/4 cup granulated sugar
- 1/4 teaspoon salt
- 3-4 tablespoons ice water

For the Coconut Cream Filling:

- 1 cup sweetened shredded coconut
- 2 cups whole milk
- 1 cup canned coconut milk
- 3/4 cup granulated sugar
- 1/3 cup cornstarch
- 1/4 teaspoon salt
- 4 large egg yolks, beaten
- 2 tablespoons unsalted butter
- 1 teaspoon vanilla extract

For the Whipped Cream Topping:

- 1 cup heavy cream
- 2 tablespoons powdered sugar
- 1/2 teaspoon vanilla extract

For Garnish:

- Toasted coconut flakes

Instructions:

1. Prepare the Pie Crust:

- In a food processor, combine the flour, cold butter cubes, sugar, and salt. Pulse until the mixture resembles coarse crumbs.
- Add ice water, one tablespoon at a time, and pulse until the dough starts to come together.
- Turn the dough out onto a floured surface and knead it a few times to form a disk. Wrap in plastic wrap and refrigerate for at least 1 hour.
- Roll out the chilled dough on a floured surface and fit it into a 9-inch pie dish. Trim and crimp the edges. Prick the bottom with a fork, and refrigerate for 30 minutes.
- Preheat the oven to 375°F (190°C). Line the chilled pie crust with parchment paper and fill it with pie weights or dried beans.
- Bake for about 15 minutes. Remove the weights and parchment, then bake for an additional 10-15 minutes or until the crust is golden brown. Allow it to cool completely.

2. Make the Coconut Cream Filling:

- In a saucepan, combine the sweetened shredded coconut, whole milk, and coconut milk. Heat over medium heat until it just starts to simmer. Remove from heat and let it steep for about 30 minutes.
- Strain the coconut milk mixture, pressing down on the coconut to extract as much flavor as possible.
- In a separate bowl, whisk together sugar, cornstarch, and salt. Gradually whisk in the beaten egg yolks.
- Gradually whisk the strained coconut milk into the sugar and egg yolk mixture.
- Return the mixture to the saucepan and cook over medium heat, stirring constantly until the mixture thickens.
- Remove from heat and stir in butter and vanilla extract until smooth. Let it cool slightly.
- Pour the coconut cream filling into the cooled pie crust. Cover the surface with plastic wrap to prevent a skin from forming. Refrigerate until set, at least 4 hours or overnight.

3. Make the Whipped Cream Topping:

- In a chilled bowl, whip the heavy cream, powdered sugar, and vanilla extract until stiff peaks form.

4. Assemble the Pie:

- Spread the whipped cream over the chilled coconut cream filling.
- Garnish with toasted coconut flakes.

5. Chill and Serve:

- Refrigerate the Coconut Cream Pie for an additional 1-2 hours to set the whipped cream.
- Slice and serve chilled. Enjoy the creamy, coconut-filled goodness!

This Coconut Cream Pie is a luscious and indulgent dessert, perfect for coconut lovers and special occasions. The combination of the flaky crust, creamy coconut filling, and billowy whipped cream is truly delightful.

Hazelnut Macarons

Ingredients:

For the Macaron Shells:

- 200g powdered sugar
- 110g almond flour
- 80g hazelnut flour
- 120g egg whites (aged, at room temperature)
- 30g granulated sugar
- A pinch of cream of tartar (optional)

For the Filling:

- Hazelnut chocolate ganache, hazelnut buttercream, or hazelnut-flavored filling of your choice

Instructions:

1. Prepare Baking Sheets:

- Line two baking sheets with parchment paper or silicone baking mats.

2. Sift Dry Ingredients:

- In a medium bowl, sift together the powdered sugar, almond flour, and hazelnut flour. Discard any larger particles that don't pass through the sieve.

3. Whip Egg Whites:

- In a clean, dry mixing bowl, beat the egg whites until foamy. Add a pinch of cream of tartar if using. Gradually add the granulated sugar while continuing to beat until stiff peaks form.

4. Macaronage:

- Gently fold the sifted dry ingredients into the whipped egg whites using a spatula. This step is called macaronage, and it's crucial to achieve the right consistency. The batter should be smooth and flow like lava.

5. Pipe Macarons:

- Transfer the batter into a piping bag fitted with a round tip. Pipe small circles (about 1.5 inches in diameter) onto the prepared baking sheets. Leave space between each macaron to allow for spreading.

6. Resting Time:
    - Let the piped macarons rest at room temperature for about 30-60 minutes until a skin forms on the surface. This helps them develop their characteristic feet during baking.

7. Preheat and Bake:
    - Preheat your oven to 300°F (150°C). Bake the macarons for 12-15 minutes, rotating the trays halfway through. They should have a crisp shell with a slightly chewy interior.

8. Cool:
    - Allow the macarons to cool completely on the baking sheets before attempting to remove them.

9. Fill:
    - Once the macarons are cool, match them up based on size and fill them with your desired hazelnut filling. Popular choices include hazelnut chocolate ganache or hazelnut buttercream.

10. Refrigerate:
    - For the best flavor and texture, refrigerate the filled macarons for at least 24 hours before serving. This allows the flavors to meld and the texture to set.

Enjoy your homemade hazelnut macarons!

Puff Pastry Palmiers

Ingredients:

- 1 sheet of puff pastry (store-bought or homemade)
- 1/2 cup granulated sugar
- 1 teaspoon ground cinnamon (optional)
- A pinch of salt (if using unsalted puff pastry)
- Egg wash (1 egg beaten with a splash of water)

Instructions:

1. Preheat the Oven:

- Preheat your oven to 375°F (190°C). Line a baking sheet with parchment paper.

2. Prepare Sugar Mixture:

- In a small bowl, combine the granulated sugar and ground cinnamon. If you're using unsalted puff pastry, you can also add a pinch of salt to balance the sweetness.

3. Roll Out Puff Pastry:

- Roll out the puff pastry sheet on a lightly floured surface to smooth out any creases. If it's not already in a rectangular shape, try to shape it into one.

4. Sprinkle Sugar Mixture:

- Evenly sprinkle the sugar mixture over the entire surface of the puff pastry.

5. Fold the Edges:

- Starting from one of the longer edges, fold the pastry inward until you reach the middle. Repeat from the opposite side, so the two folds meet in the center.

6. Fold Again:

- Fold the pastry in half along the center line, bringing the two folded edges together.

7. Slice Into Palmiers:

- Using a sharp knife, slice the folded pastry into 1/2-inch to 1-inch slices. Lay each slice on the prepared baking sheet with some space between them.

8. Brush with Egg Wash:

- Lightly brush each palmier with the egg wash. This will give them a golden color when baked.

9. Bake:

- Bake in the preheated oven for 12-15 minutes or until the palmiers are puffed and golden brown. Keep an eye on them to prevent burning.

10. Cool:

- Allow the palmiers to cool on the baking sheet for a few minutes, then transfer them to a wire rack to cool completely.

These Puff Pastry Palmiers are delightful on their own or can be served with a cup of coffee or tea. Enjoy the crispy, caramelized layers!

S'mores Brownies

Ingredients:

For the Brownie Layer:

- 1 cup (2 sticks) unsalted butter
- 2 cups granulated sugar
- 4 large eggs
- 1 teaspoon vanilla extract
- 1 cup all-purpose flour
- 1/2 cup cocoa powder
- 1/4 teaspoon salt

For the S'mores Topping:

- 2 cups mini marshmallows
- 1 cup chocolate chips or chopped chocolate
- 1 cup graham cracker crumbs

Instructions:

1. Preheat the Oven:

- Preheat your oven to 350°F (175°C). Grease and line a 9x13-inch baking pan with parchment paper, leaving an overhang for easy removal.

2. Prepare the Brownie Batter:

- In a saucepan or microwave, melt the butter. In a large mixing bowl, combine the melted butter with sugar, eggs, and vanilla extract. Mix well.
- Sift in the flour, cocoa powder, and salt. Mix until just combined. Do not overmix.

3. Bake the Brownies:

- Pour the brownie batter into the prepared baking pan and spread it evenly. Bake in the preheated oven for about 25-30 minutes or until a toothpick inserted into the center comes out with moist crumbs (not wet batter).

4. Add S'mores Topping:

- Sprinkle the mini marshmallows evenly over the hot brownies, followed by the chocolate chips or chopped chocolate. Return the pan to the oven for an additional 5-7 minutes or until the marshmallows are golden and puffed.

5. Toast the Marshmallows:

- If you want a toasted marshmallow topping, you can use a kitchen torch to carefully toast the marshmallows. Alternatively, you can place the pan under the broiler for a brief moment, but be watchful to prevent burning.

6. Add Graham Cracker Crumbs:

- Sprinkle the graham cracker crumbs over the melted chocolate and marshmallow layer.

7. Cool and Slice:

- Allow the S'mores Brownies to cool completely in the pan on a wire rack. Once cooled, use the parchment paper overhang to lift the brownies out of the pan. Place on a cutting board and slice into squares.

8. Serve:

- Serve the S'mores Brownies and enjoy the gooey, chocolatey, marshmallow goodness!

These brownies are a delightful twist on the classic S'mores, combining the rich flavors of brownies with the nostalgic taste of campfire treats.

Apple Cider Donuts

Ingredients:

For the Donuts:

- 2 cups apple cider
- 3 1/2 cups all-purpose flour
- 1 1/2 teaspoons baking powder
- 1 1/2 teaspoons baking soda
- 1/2 teaspoon salt
- 2 teaspoons ground cinnamon
- 1/2 teaspoon ground nutmeg
- 1/2 cup unsalted butter, softened
- 1 cup granulated sugar
- 2 large eggs
- 1 teaspoon vanilla extract

For the Cinnamon Sugar Coating:

- 1 cup granulated sugar
- 1 tablespoon ground cinnamon
- 1/2 cup unsalted butter, melted

Instructions:

1. Reduce Apple Cider:

    - In a saucepan over medium heat, simmer the apple cider until it reduces to about 1 cup. Allow it to cool.

2. Preheat the Oven:

    - Preheat your oven to 350°F (175°C). Grease your donut pans.

3. Mix Dry Ingredients:

    - In a medium bowl, whisk together the flour, baking powder, baking soda, salt, cinnamon, and nutmeg.

4. Cream Butter and Sugar:

    - In a large bowl, cream together the softened butter and sugar until light and fluffy.

5. Add Eggs and Vanilla:
   - Beat in the eggs, one at a time, then add the vanilla extract, mixing well.

6. Combine Wet and Dry Ingredients:
   - Add the reduced apple cider to the butter and sugar mixture. Mix until well combined.
   - Gradually add the dry ingredients to the wet ingredients, mixing until just combined. Do not overmix.

7. Fill Donut Pans:
   - Spoon the batter into greased donut pans, filling each cavity about 2/3 full.

8. Bake:
   - Bake in the preheated oven for 12-15 minutes or until a toothpick inserted into the center of a donut comes out clean.

9. Coat with Cinnamon Sugar:
   - While the donuts are baking, prepare the cinnamon sugar coating. In a bowl, combine granulated sugar and ground cinnamon.
   - Once the donuts are done and still warm, dip each donut into the melted butter and then roll it in the cinnamon sugar mixture until coated.

10. Serve:
    - Allow the donuts to cool slightly before serving. Enjoy these delicious apple cider donuts with a cup of coffee or tea!

These apple cider donuts are a perfect autumn treat, capturing the flavors of the season in a delightful and comforting dessert.

Mint Chocolate Chip Ice Cream Sandwiches

Ingredients:

For the Cookies:

- 1 cup unsalted butter, softened
- 1 cup granulated sugar
- 1 large egg
- 1 teaspoon vanilla extract
- 2 cups all-purpose flour
- 1/2 cup cocoa powder
- 1/2 teaspoon baking powder
- 1/2 teaspoon baking soda
- 1/4 teaspoon salt
- 1/2 cup mini chocolate chips
- Fresh mint leaves (optional for added flavor)

For the Mint Chocolate Chip Ice Cream:

- 2 cups heavy cream
- 1 cup whole milk
- 3/4 cup granulated sugar
- 1 teaspoon peppermint extract
- Green food coloring (optional)
- 1 cup mini chocolate chips

Instructions:

For the Cookies:

Preheat the Oven:
- Preheat your oven to 350°F (175°C). Line baking sheets with parchment paper.

Cream Butter and Sugar:
- In a large bowl, cream together the softened butter and sugar until light and fluffy.

Add Egg and Vanilla:
- Beat in the egg and vanilla extract until well combined.

Combine Dry Ingredients:
- In a separate bowl, whisk together the flour, cocoa powder, baking powder, baking soda, and salt.

Mix Wet and Dry Ingredients:

- Gradually add the dry ingredients to the wet ingredients, mixing until just combined. Fold in the mini chocolate chips and chopped fresh mint leaves if using.

Form Cookies:
- Drop rounded tablespoons of dough onto the prepared baking sheets, leaving space between each cookie. Flatten slightly with the back of a spoon.

Bake:
- Bake in the preheated oven for 10-12 minutes or until the edges are set. Allow the cookies to cool on the baking sheets for a few minutes before transferring them to a wire rack to cool completely.

For the Mint Chocolate Chip Ice Cream:

Prepare Ice Cream Base:
- In a bowl, whisk together the heavy cream, whole milk, granulated sugar, and peppermint extract until the sugar is dissolved. Add green food coloring if desired.

Churn Ice Cream:
- Pour the mixture into an ice cream maker and churn according to the manufacturer's instructions. In the last few minutes of churning, add the mini chocolate chips.

Freeze:
- Transfer the churned ice cream to a lidded container and freeze until firm.

Assemble Ice Cream Sandwiches:

Match Cookies:
- Once the cookies and ice cream are completely cooled and frozen, match cookies of similar sizes.

Assemble:
- Scoop a generous amount of mint chocolate chip ice cream onto the bottom side of one cookie and press another cookie on top to create a sandwich.

Freeze Again:
- Place the assembled ice cream sandwiches in the freezer for at least 1-2 hours to allow the ice cream to firm up.

Serve and Enjoy:
- Serve these mint chocolate chip ice cream sandwiches and enjoy the delightful combination of cool mint and rich chocolate!

These ice cream sandwiches are a delicious and fun dessert that's sure to be a hit, especially on warm days.

Peanut Butter Cupcakes

Ingredients:

For the Peanut Butter Cupcakes:

- 1 1/2 cups all-purpose flour
- 1 1/2 teaspoons baking powder
- 1/4 teaspoon salt
- 1/2 cup unsalted butter, softened
- 1 cup granulated sugar
- 2 large eggs
- 1 teaspoon vanilla extract
- 1/2 cup creamy peanut butter
- 3/4 cup whole milk

For the Peanut Butter Frosting:

- 1/2 cup unsalted butter, softened
- 1 cup creamy peanut butter
- 2 cups powdered sugar
- 1 teaspoon vanilla extract
- 3-4 tablespoons whole milk

Instructions:

For the Peanut Butter Cupcakes:

Preheat the Oven:
- Preheat your oven to 350°F (175°C). Line a cupcake pan with paper liners.

Combine Dry Ingredients:
- In a bowl, whisk together the flour, baking powder, and salt. Set aside.

Cream Butter and Sugar:
- In a large bowl, cream together the softened butter and sugar until light and fluffy.

Add Eggs and Vanilla:
- Beat in the eggs one at a time, then add the vanilla extract and continue mixing.

Add Peanut Butter:
- Mix in the creamy peanut butter until well combined.

Alternate Dry Ingredients and Milk:

- Gradually add the dry ingredients to the wet ingredients, alternating with the milk. Begin and end with the dry ingredients, mixing until just combined.

Fill Cupcake Liners:
- Divide the batter evenly among the cupcake liners, filling each about 2/3 full.

Bake:
- Bake in the preheated oven for 18-20 minutes or until a toothpick inserted into the center comes out clean. Allow the cupcakes to cool in the pan for a few minutes before transferring them to a wire rack to cool completely.

For the Peanut Butter Frosting:

Cream Butter and Peanut Butter:
- In a large bowl, cream together the softened butter and creamy peanut butter until smooth.

Add Vanilla:
- Add the vanilla extract and mix well.

Gradually Add Powdered Sugar:
- Gradually add the powdered sugar, one cup at a time, and beat until well combined.

Adjust Consistency:
- Add whole milk, one tablespoon at a time, until you reach your desired frosting consistency.

Assemble:

Frost Cupcakes:
- Once the cupcakes are completely cooled, frost them with the peanut butter frosting using a piping bag or a spatula.

Optional: Garnish:
- Garnish the cupcakes with chopped peanuts, chocolate shavings, or a drizzle of melted chocolate if desired.

Serve and Enjoy:
- Serve these delicious peanut butter cupcakes and enjoy the rich and nutty flavor!

These peanut butter cupcakes are a wonderful treat for any occasion, and the creamy peanut butter frosting adds the perfect finishing touch.

Cranberry Orange Scones

Ingredients:

For the Scones:

- 2 cups all-purpose flour
- 1/4 cup granulated sugar
- 1 tablespoon baking powder
- 1/2 teaspoon salt
- 1/2 cup unsalted butter, cold and cut into small pieces
- 1/2 cup dried cranberries
- Zest of 1 orange
- 1/2 cup milk
- 1/4 cup fresh orange juice
- 1 teaspoon vanilla extract

For the Orange Glaze:

- 1 cup powdered sugar
- 2 tablespoons fresh orange juice
- Zest of 1 orange (optional)

Instructions:

For the Scones:

    Preheat the Oven:
- Preheat your oven to 400°F (200°C). Line a baking sheet with parchment paper.

    Combine Dry Ingredients:
- In a large bowl, whisk together the flour, sugar, baking powder, and salt.

    Cut in Butter:
- Add the cold, diced butter to the dry ingredients. Use a pastry cutter or your fingertips to cut the butter into the flour mixture until it resembles coarse crumbs.

    Add Cranberries and Orange Zest:
- Stir in the dried cranberries and orange zest.

    Combine Wet Ingredients:
- In a separate bowl, mix together the milk, fresh orange juice, and vanilla extract.

Mix Wet and Dry Ingredients:
- Add the wet ingredients to the dry ingredients and stir until just combined. Do not overmix; the dough should be slightly sticky.

Shape the Dough:
- Turn the dough out onto a floured surface and gently knead it a few times. Pat the dough into a circle about 1 inch thick.

Cut Into Wedges:
- Using a sharp knife or a bench scraper, cut the dough into 8 wedges.

Bake:
- Transfer the scones to the prepared baking sheet. Bake in the preheated oven for 15-18 minutes or until the edges are golden brown.

Cool:
- Allow the scones to cool on the baking sheet for a few minutes before transferring them to a wire rack to cool completely.

For the Orange Glaze:

Prepare Glaze:
- In a small bowl, whisk together the powdered sugar and fresh orange juice until smooth.

Drizzle Glaze:
- Once the scones are cooled, drizzle the orange glaze over the top. Optionally, sprinkle additional orange zest on top of the glaze for extra flavor and decoration.

Let Glaze Set:
- Allow the glaze to set before serving.

Serve and Enjoy:

Serve these cranberry orange scones with a cup of tea or coffee for a delightful breakfast or afternoon treat. The combination of tart cranberries and bright orange flavors makes these scones a delicious and festive option for any occasion.

Dark Chocolate Torte

Ingredients:

For the Torte:

- 8 ounces (about 225g) high-quality dark chocolate, finely chopped
- 1 cup (2 sticks) unsalted butter
- 1 cup granulated sugar
- 1/2 cup all-purpose flour
- 1/4 cup unsweetened cocoa powder
- 1/4 teaspoon salt
- 5 large eggs
- 1 teaspoon vanilla extract

For Serving (Optional):

- Powdered sugar for dusting
- Fresh berries or a berry compote
- Whipped cream or vanilla ice cream

Instructions:

1. Preheat the Oven:

- Preheat your oven to 325°F (163°C). Grease a 9-inch round cake pan and line the bottom with parchment paper.

2. Melt Chocolate and Butter:

- In a heatproof bowl, melt the finely chopped dark chocolate and butter together. You can do this using a double boiler or by melting in short bursts in the microwave, stirring frequently until smooth. Allow it to cool slightly.

3. Prepare Dry Ingredients:

- In a separate bowl, sift together the all-purpose flour, cocoa powder, and salt. Set aside.

4. Mix Wet Ingredients:

- In a large bowl, whisk together the sugar and eggs until well combined. Add the vanilla extract and mix.

5. Combine Wet and Dry Ingredients:
    - Gradually fold the melted chocolate and butter mixture into the egg and sugar mixture until well combined.
    - Gently fold in the sifted dry ingredients until just incorporated. Be careful not to overmix.

6. Bake:
    - Pour the batter into the prepared cake pan and smooth the top with a spatula.
    - Bake in the preheated oven for about 35-40 minutes or until a toothpick inserted into the center comes out with moist crumbs. The torte should have a slightly cracked top.

7. Cool:
    - Allow the torte to cool in the pan for about 15 minutes, then transfer it to a wire rack to cool completely.

8. Serve:
    - Dust the cooled dark chocolate torte with powdered sugar before serving.
    - Optionally, serve slices with fresh berries, a berry compote, whipped cream, or vanilla ice cream.

9. Enjoy:
    - Slice and enjoy this rich and delightful dark chocolate torte!

This dark chocolate torte is a sophisticated dessert that's perfect for special occasions or when you're craving an indulgent chocolate treat. The combination of deep, dark chocolate and a dense, moist texture makes it a true delight for chocolate enthusiasts.

Raspberry Swirl Cheesecake Bars

Ingredients:

For the Crust:

- 1 1/2 cups graham cracker crumbs
- 1/4 cup granulated sugar
- 1/2 cup unsalted butter, melted

For the Cheesecake Filling:

- 16 ounces (2 packages) cream cheese, softened
- 1 cup granulated sugar
- 3 large eggs
- 1 teaspoon vanilla extract
- 1/2 cup sour cream

For the Raspberry Swirl:

- 1 cup fresh or frozen raspberries
- 2 tablespoons granulated sugar
- 1 tablespoon water
- 1 teaspoon cornstarch

Instructions:

For the Crust:

> Preheat the Oven:
> - Preheat your oven to 325°F (163°C). Line a 9x9-inch baking pan with parchment paper, leaving an overhang on the sides for easy removal.
>
> Make the Crust:
> - In a bowl, combine the graham cracker crumbs, sugar, and melted butter. Press the mixture firmly into the bottom of the prepared pan to form an even crust.
>
> Bake the Crust:
> - Bake the crust in the preheated oven for 10 minutes. Remove and let it cool while preparing the filling.

For the Cheesecake Filling:

> Prepare Cheesecake Batter:

- In a large mixing bowl, beat the softened cream cheese until smooth. Add the sugar and beat until well combined.

Add Eggs and Vanilla:
- Add the eggs one at a time, beating well after each addition. Mix in the vanilla extract.

Incorporate Sour Cream:
- Gently fold in the sour cream until the batter is smooth and well combined.

For the Raspberry Swirl:

Prepare Raspberry Sauce:
- In a small saucepan, combine the raspberries, sugar, water, and cornstarch. Cook over medium heat, stirring continuously until the raspberries break down and the mixture thickens.

Strain the Sauce:
- Strain the raspberry mixture through a fine-mesh sieve to remove seeds, pressing down to extract as much liquid as possible.

Assemble and Bake:

Layer the Cheesecake:
- Pour the cheesecake batter over the cooled crust in the baking pan.

Add Raspberry Swirl:
- Spoon dollops of the strained raspberry sauce onto the cheesecake batter. Use a knife or toothpick to swirl the raspberry sauce into the cheesecake.

Bake:
- Bake in the preheated oven for 35-40 minutes or until the center is set. The edges should be slightly golden.

Cool and Chill:
- Allow the cheesecake bars to cool in the pan, then refrigerate for at least 4 hours or overnight to set.

Serve and Enjoy:

Slice:
- Use the parchment paper overhang to lift the cheesecake from the pan. Place it on a cutting board and slice into bars.

Serve:
- Serve the Raspberry Swirl Cheesecake Bars chilled. Optionally, garnish with fresh raspberries or a dusting of powdered sugar.

Enjoy:
- Enjoy these delicious and tangy cheesecake bars with the raspberry swirl!

These Raspberry Swirl Cheesecake Bars are a perfect combination of creamy, tangy, and sweet flavors—a delightful treat for any occasion.

Classic Danish Pastry

Ingredients:

For the Dough:

- 1 cup (240ml) whole milk, lukewarm
- 2 1/4 teaspoons (1 packet) active dry yeast
- 1/4 cup (50g) granulated sugar
- 3 1/4 cups (400g) all-purpose flour, sifted
- 1/2 teaspoon salt
- 1 cup (2 sticks or 225g) unsalted butter, cold

For Laminating:

- Additional 1 cup (2 sticks or 225g) unsalted butter, cold

For Filling (Optional):

- Fruit preserves, pastry cream, almond paste, or other fillings of your choice

For Glaze:

- 1 cup powdered sugar
- 2 tablespoons milk or water
- 1/2 teaspoon vanilla extract

Instructions:

1. Activate the Yeast:

- In a bowl, combine lukewarm milk and sugar. Sprinkle the yeast over the mixture and let it sit for about 5-10 minutes until foamy.

2. Mix Dry Ingredients:

- In a large bowl, sift together the flour and salt.

3. Make the Dough:

- Add the yeast mixture to the flour and mix until a dough forms. Knead the dough on a lightly floured surface until smooth.

4. Chill the Dough:

- Wrap the dough in plastic wrap and refrigerate for at least 2 hours or overnight.

5. Laminating:
   - Roll out the cold dough on a floured surface into a rectangle.
   - Flatten the additional cold butter into a rectangle and place it on two-thirds of the rolled-out dough.
   - Fold the uncovered third over the butter, then fold the remaining third over the top (similar to a letter fold).
   - Roll out the dough again and repeat the folding process. Repeat this process 3-4 times, chilling the dough between each fold.

6. Shape the Danish:
   - Roll out the laminated dough into the desired shape (twists, braids, squares, etc.).
   - Add your chosen filling, leaving space around the edges.

7. Proof:
   - Allow the shaped pastries to proof for about 1-2 hours, or until they are puffy and visibly risen.

8. Bake:
   - Preheat your oven to 400°F (200°C) and bake the pastries for 15-20 minutes or until golden brown.

9. Make the Glaze:
   - In a bowl, whisk together powdered sugar, milk (or water), and vanilla extract until smooth.

10. Glaze and Enjoy:
    - Once the pastries are cooled, drizzle the glaze over the top.
    - Serve and enjoy your homemade classic Danish pastries!

Feel free to experiment with different fillings and shapes to create a variety of delicious Danish pastries. Whether you prefer a fruit-filled treat or a classic cinnamon twist, these pastries are sure to be a hit.

Pistachio Baklava

Ingredients:

For the Baklava:

- 1 package (about 16 ounces) phyllo dough, thawed
- 1 1/2 cups unsalted pistachios, finely chopped
- 1 cup unsalted butter, melted
- 1 cup granulated sugar
- 1 teaspoon ground cinnamon

For the Syrup:

- 1 cup water
- 1 cup granulated sugar
- 1/2 cup honey
- 1 tablespoon lemon juice
- 1 teaspoon rose water (optional, for flavor)

Instructions:

1. Preheat the Oven:

   - Preheat your oven to 325°F (163°C). Grease a 9x13-inch baking dish.

2. Prepare the Pistachios:

   - Finely chop the unsalted pistachios. You can use a food processor for this, but be careful not to over-process; you want a mix of finely chopped and slightly larger pieces for texture.

3. Layer the Phyllo Dough:

   - Unroll the phyllo dough and place it between two sheets of plastic wrap or a damp kitchen towel to prevent it from drying out.
   - Brush the bottom of the baking dish with melted butter.
   - Place one sheet of phyllo dough in the dish and brush it with melted butter. Repeat this process, layering about 8-10 sheets.

4. Add the Pistachio Filling:

   - Sprinkle a layer of finely chopped pistachios over the phyllo sheets.

- Add another layer of phyllo sheets, brushing each layer with melted butter. Repeat the process until you've used half of the phyllo sheets.
- Sprinkle another layer of chopped pistachios.

5. Finish the Layering:

- Continue layering the remaining phyllo sheets, brushing each layer with melted butter.
- Finish with a layer of chopped pistachios on top.

6. Cut into Diamonds:

- Using a sharp knife, carefully cut the baklava into diamond or square shapes. Be sure to cut all the way through the layers.

7. Bake:

- Bake in the preheated oven for 40-50 minutes or until the baklava is golden brown and crisp.

8. Make the Syrup:

- While the baklava is baking, prepare the syrup. In a saucepan, combine water, sugar, honey, lemon juice, and rose water (if using). Bring to a boil, then reduce the heat and simmer for about 10-15 minutes until the syrup slightly thickens.

9. Pour the Syrup:

- Once the baklava is out of the oven, immediately pour the hot syrup evenly over the hot baklava.

10. Cool and Serve:

- Allow the baklava to cool completely before serving. This allows the phyllo layers to absorb the syrup.
- Serve and enjoy this sweet and nutty pistachio baklava!

Pistachio baklava is a wonderful dessert that combines the flakiness of phyllo dough with the richness of pistachios and the sweetness of honey syrup. It's a delightful treat to share with family and friends.

Strawberry Rhubarb Pie

Ingredients:

For the Pie Crust:

- 2 1/2 cups all-purpose flour
- 1 cup unsalted butter, chilled and cut into small cubes
- 1 teaspoon salt
- 1 tablespoon granulated sugar
- 1/4 to 1/2 cup ice water

For the Filling:

- 3 cups fresh rhubarb, chopped into 1/2-inch pieces
- 3 cups fresh strawberries, hulled and halved (or quartered if large)
- 1 cup granulated sugar (adjust based on sweetness of fruit)
- 1/4 cup cornstarch
- 1 tablespoon lemon juice
- 1 teaspoon vanilla extract
- 1/2 teaspoon ground cinnamon (optional)
- 1 tablespoon butter, cut into small pieces

Instructions:

1. Prepare the Pie Crust:

- In a large bowl, combine the flour, salt, and sugar. Add the chilled butter cubes.
- Using a pastry cutter or your fingers, work the butter into the flour until it resembles coarse crumbs.
- Gradually add ice water, a tablespoon at a time, and mix until the dough just comes together. Divide the dough in half, shape each half into a disk, wrap in plastic wrap, and refrigerate for at least 1 hour.

2. Preheat the Oven:

- Preheat your oven to 400°F (200°C).

3. Roll Out the Crust:

- On a lightly floured surface, roll out one disk of the pie crust to fit a 9-inch pie dish. Place the rolled-out crust in the pie dish and trim the edges.

4. Prepare the Filling:
   - In a large bowl, combine the chopped rhubarb, halved strawberries, sugar, cornstarch, lemon juice, vanilla extract, and ground cinnamon (if using). Toss the filling until the fruit is evenly coated.

5. Fill the Pie:
   - Pour the strawberry rhubarb filling into the prepared pie crust. Dot the filling with small pieces of butter.

6. Roll Out the Top Crust:
   - Roll out the second disk of pie crust and place it over the filling. Trim and crimp the edges to seal the pie.

7. Vent the Pie:
   - Cut a few slits or a decorative pattern in the top crust to allow steam to escape.

8. Bake:
   - Place the pie on a baking sheet to catch any drips and bake in the preheated oven for about 45-50 minutes or until the crust is golden brown, and the filling is bubbly.

9. Cool:
   - Allow the strawberry rhubarb pie to cool on a wire rack for at least 2 hours before serving. This allows the filling to set.

10. Serve:
    - Serve the pie slices with a scoop of vanilla ice cream or a dollop of whipped cream if desired.

Enjoy the delightful combination of sweet strawberries and tart rhubarb in this classic strawberry rhubarb pie!

Chocolate Cherry Tart

Ingredients:

For the Tart Crust:

- 1 1/4 cups all-purpose flour
- 1/4 cup unsweetened cocoa powder
- 1/2 cup unsalted butter, chilled and cut into small pieces
- 1/4 cup granulated sugar
- 1/4 teaspoon salt
- 1 large egg yolk
- 2 tablespoons ice water

For the Chocolate Ganache:

- 1 cup heavy cream
- 8 ounces bittersweet chocolate, finely chopped

For the Cherry Filling:

- 2 cups fresh cherries, pitted and halved
- 1/4 cup granulated sugar
- 1 tablespoon cornstarch
- 1 tablespoon lemon juice
- 1/2 teaspoon vanilla extract

Instructions:

For the Tart Crust:

Prepare the Crust:
- In a food processor, combine the flour, cocoa powder, butter, sugar, and salt. Pulse until the mixture resembles coarse crumbs.

Add Egg Yolk and Water:
- Add the egg yolk and pulse again. Gradually add ice water, one tablespoon at a time, and pulse until the dough starts to come together.

Form the Dough:
- Turn the dough out onto a lightly floured surface and knead it gently until it forms a ball. Flatten the ball into a disk, wrap it in plastic wrap, and refrigerate for at least 30 minutes.

Roll Out the Crust:
- Preheat your oven to 375°F (190°C). On a floured surface, roll out the chilled dough to fit a tart pan. Press the dough into the pan, trimming any excess.

Chill Again:
- Place the tart pan in the refrigerator for another 15-20 minutes.

Blind Bake:
- Line the chilled crust with parchment paper and fill it with pie weights or dried beans. Blind bake for about 15 minutes. Remove the weights and parchment, then bake for an additional 5 minutes until the crust is set. Allow it to cool.

For the Chocolate Ganache:

Heat Cream:
- In a saucepan, heat the heavy cream over medium heat until it just begins to simmer.

Pour over Chocolate:
- Place the finely chopped chocolate in a heatproof bowl. Pour the hot cream over the chocolate and let it sit for a minute.

Whisk:
- Stir the chocolate and cream together until smooth and well combined. Let it cool slightly.

Pour into Crust:
- Pour the chocolate ganache into the cooled tart crust. Spread it evenly with a spatula.

For the Cherry Filling:

Prepare Cherries:
- In a bowl, toss the halved cherries with sugar, cornstarch, lemon juice, and vanilla extract until well coated.

Cook Cherries:
- In a saucepan, cook the cherry mixture over medium heat until the cherries release their juices and the mixture thickens slightly (about 5-7 minutes).

Cool:
- Allow the cherry filling to cool slightly, then spoon it over the chocolate ganache in the tart.

Chill:

- Refrigerate the chocolate cherry tart for at least 2 hours or until the ganache is set.

Serve:
- Slice and serve the chocolate cherry tart, optionally garnishing with whipped cream or a dusting of cocoa powder.

This chocolate cherry tart is a luscious and indulgent dessert that's perfect for special occasions or when you're craving a combination of rich chocolate and sweet-tart cherries. Enjoy!

Lemon Lavender Shortbread Cookies

Ingredients:

For the Shortbread Cookies:

- 1 cup unsalted butter, softened
- 1/2 cup granulated sugar
- 2 cups all-purpose flour
- Zest of 2 lemons
- 1 tablespoon dried culinary lavender buds (culinary-grade)

For the Lemon Lavender Glaze:

- 1 cup powdered sugar
- 2 tablespoons fresh lemon juice
- 1 teaspoon dried culinary lavender buds (culinary-grade)
- Additional lemon zest for garnish (optional)

Instructions:

For the Shortbread Cookies:

    Preheat the Oven:
- Preheat your oven to 325°F (163°C). Line a baking sheet with parchment paper.

    Cream Butter and Sugar:
- In a large bowl, cream together the softened butter and granulated sugar until light and fluffy.

    Add Flour, Lemon Zest, and Lavender:
- Gradually add the all-purpose flour, lemon zest, and dried lavender buds to the creamed mixture. Mix until the dough comes together.

    Shape the Cookies:
- Divide the dough into two equal portions. Roll each portion into a log shape, about 1.5 inches in diameter. Wrap the logs in plastic wrap and refrigerate for at least 1 hour or until firm.

    Slice and Bake:
- Once the dough is chilled, slice it into rounds about 1/4 to 1/2 inch thick. Place the slices on the prepared baking sheet, leaving space between each cookie.

    Bake:

- Bake in the preheated oven for 12-15 minutes or until the edges of the cookies are lightly golden. Keep a close eye to prevent over-baking.

Cool:
- Allow the cookies to cool on the baking sheet for a few minutes before transferring them to a wire rack to cool completely.

For the Lemon Lavender Glaze:

Prepare the Glaze:
- In a small saucepan, heat the lemon juice and dried lavender buds over low heat until it simmers. Remove from heat and let the lavender steep in the juice for about 5 minutes. Strain out the lavender buds and allow the infused juice to cool.

Make the Glaze:
- In a bowl, whisk together the powdered sugar and the infused lemon juice until you have a smooth glaze.

Glaze the Cookies:
- Once the cookies are completely cooled, drizzle the glaze over the top of each cookie. You can also dip the tops of the cookies into the glaze.

Optional Garnish:
- Optionally, garnish the glazed cookies with a sprinkle of additional dried lavender buds and lemon zest.

Allow the Glaze to Set:
- Allow the glaze to set before serving. This may take about 1-2 hours.

These lemon lavender shortbread cookies are perfect for tea time or as a light and fragrant dessert. Enjoy the delicate balance of citrus and floral notes in each crumbly bite!

Vanilla Bean Madeleines

Ingredients:

- 1 cup (2 sticks) unsalted butter, melted and cooled
- 1 vanilla bean pod
- 1 cup all-purpose flour
- 1/2 teaspoon baking powder
- 1/4 teaspoon salt
- 3 large eggs, at room temperature
- 1 cup granulated sugar
- 1 teaspoon pure vanilla extract
- Powdered sugar for dusting (optional)

Instructions:

1. Preheat the Oven:

- Preheat your oven to 375°F (190°C). Grease and flour madeleine molds or use a non-stick madeleine pan.

2. Prepare the Vanilla Bean:

- Split the vanilla bean pod lengthwise using a sharp knife. Scrape out the seeds using the back of the knife.

3. Make the Brown Butter:

- In a saucepan, melt the butter over medium heat. Once melted, continue to cook until the butter turns golden brown and has a nutty aroma. Remove from heat and let it cool slightly.

4. Sift Dry Ingredients:

- In a bowl, sift together the all-purpose flour, baking powder, and salt.

5. Whisk Eggs and Sugar:

- In a separate bowl, whisk together the eggs and granulated sugar until the mixture is pale and thick.

6. Add Vanilla:

- Add the vanilla bean seeds and vanilla extract to the egg mixture. Mix until well combined.

7. Fold in Dry Ingredients:
    - Gently fold in the sifted dry ingredients into the egg mixture until just combined.

8. Add Brown Butter:
    - Pour the cooled brown butter into the batter and gently fold until smooth.

9. Chill the Batter:
    - Cover the batter and refrigerate for at least 1 hour or until it firms up.

10. Fill Madeleine Molds:
    - Spoon the chilled batter into the prepared madeleine molds, filling each mold about 3/4 full.

11. Bake:
    - Bake in the preheated oven for 10-12 minutes or until the edges of the madeleines are golden brown and the centers spring back when lightly touched.

12. Cool and Dust with Powdered Sugar:
    - Allow the madeleines to cool in the pan for a few minutes before transferring them to a wire rack to cool completely. Dust with powdered sugar before serving if desired.

13. Serve:
    - Serve these delicate vanilla bean madeleines with a cup of tea or coffee and enjoy their light, buttery goodness.

These vanilla bean madeleines are not only delicious but also make for an elegant and charming treat. The addition of vanilla bean seeds adds a delightful speckled appearance and enhances the overall flavor.

Chocolate Hazelnut Biscotti

Ingredients:

- 1 cup (about 150g) hazelnuts, toasted and chopped
- 2 cups all-purpose flour
- 1/2 cup unsweetened cocoa powder
- 1 teaspoon baking soda
- 1/4 teaspoon salt
- 1/2 cup unsalted butter, softened
- 1 cup granulated sugar
- 2 large eggs
- 1 teaspoon vanilla extract
- 1/2 cup semisweet chocolate chips or chunks

Instructions:

1. Preheat the Oven:

    - Preheat your oven to 350°F (175°C). Line a baking sheet with parchment paper.

2. Toast and Chop Hazelnuts:

    - Spread the hazelnuts on a baking sheet and toast in the preheated oven for about 10 minutes or until fragrant. Allow them to cool slightly, then chop coarsely.

3. Mix Dry Ingredients:

    - In a bowl, whisk together the flour, cocoa powder, baking soda, and salt.

4. Cream Butter and Sugar:

    - In a separate bowl, cream together the softened butter and sugar until light and fluffy.

5. Add Eggs and Vanilla:

    - Add the eggs one at a time, beating well after each addition. Mix in the vanilla extract.

6. Combine Wet and Dry Ingredients:

- Gradually add the dry ingredients to the wet ingredients, mixing until just combined.

7. Fold in Hazelnuts and Chocolate:
    - Gently fold in the toasted and chopped hazelnuts, and chocolate chips or chunks until evenly distributed in the dough.

8. Shape the Dough:
    - Divide the dough in half. On a lightly floured surface, shape each portion into a log about 12 inches long and 2 inches wide. Place the logs on the prepared baking sheet, leaving space between them.

9. Bake:
    - Bake in the preheated oven for 25-30 minutes or until the logs are set. Allow them to cool on the baking sheet for 15 minutes.

10. Slice the Biscotti:
    - Using a serrated knife, slice the logs diagonally into 1/2-inch-wide slices.

11. Second Bake:
    - Place the biscotti slices cut-side down on the baking sheet. Bake for an additional 10-12 minutes or until the biscotti are dry and crisp. Flip them halfway through for even baking.

12. Cool:
    - Allow the chocolate hazelnut biscotti to cool completely on a wire rack.

13. Serve and Enjoy:
    - Once cooled, these biscotti are ready to be served. Enjoy them dipped in coffee, tea, or your favorite beverage.

These chocolate hazelnut biscotti are a delicious treat with a perfect balance of chocolate richness and nutty flavor. They store well in an airtight container and make a lovely homemade gift.

Raspberry Chocolate Ganache Tart

Ingredients:

For the Tart Crust:

- 1 1/2 cups graham cracker crumbs
- 1/3 cup unsalted butter, melted
- 1/4 cup granulated sugar

For the Chocolate Ganache:

- 1 cup heavy cream
- 8 ounces semisweet or bittersweet chocolate, finely chopped
- 2 tablespoons unsalted butter, at room temperature

For Topping:

- 1 pint fresh raspberries
- Powdered sugar for dusting (optional)

Instructions:

For the Tart Crust:

Preheat the Oven:
- Preheat your oven to 350°F (175°C).

Prepare the Crust:
- In a bowl, combine the graham cracker crumbs, melted butter, and granulated sugar. Mix until the crumbs are evenly coated.

Press into Tart Pan:
- Press the mixture into the bottom and up the sides of a 9-inch tart pan with a removable bottom.

Bake:
- Bake the crust in the preheated oven for about 8-10 minutes or until set. Allow it to cool completely.

For the Chocolate Ganache:

Heat the Cream:
- In a saucepan, heat the heavy cream over medium heat until it just begins to simmer. Do not boil.

Add Chocolate:
- Place the finely chopped chocolate in a heatproof bowl. Pour the hot cream over the chocolate and let it sit for a minute.

Whisk:
- Stir the chocolate and cream together until smooth and well combined.

Add Butter:
- Add the room temperature butter and whisk until the ganache is glossy and smooth.

Cool:
- Allow the ganache to cool slightly, but make sure it is still pourable.

Assembling the Tart:

Pour Ganache:
- Pour the chocolate ganache into the cooled tart crust. Smooth the top with a spatula.

Chill:
- Place the tart in the refrigerator to set the ganache for at least 2 hours or until firm.

Top with Raspberries:
- Once the ganache has set, arrange fresh raspberries on top of the tart.

Dust with Powdered Sugar:
- Optionally, dust the tart with powdered sugar for a finishing touch.

Serve and Enjoy:
- Slice and serve this delightful Raspberry Chocolate Ganache Tart. It's perfect for special occasions or when you're craving a luxurious chocolate treat with the bright addition of raspberries.

This tart is a wonderful combination of smooth chocolate ganache and the vibrant taste of fresh raspberries, creating a dessert that's both elegant and delicious.

Oatmeal Raisin Cookies

Ingredients:

- 1 cup (2 sticks) unsalted butter, softened
- 1 cup packed light brown sugar
- 1/2 cup granulated sugar
- 2 large eggs
- 1 teaspoon vanilla extract
- 1 1/2 cups all-purpose flour
- 1 teaspoon baking soda
- 1 teaspoon ground cinnamon
- 1/2 teaspoon salt
- 3 cups old-fashioned oats
- 1 cup raisins

Instructions:

1. Preheat the Oven:

    - Preheat your oven to 350°F (175°C). Line baking sheets with parchment paper.

2. Cream Butter and Sugars:

    - In a large bowl, cream together the softened butter, brown sugar, and granulated sugar until light and fluffy.

3. Add Eggs and Vanilla:

    - Add the eggs one at a time, beating well after each addition. Mix in the vanilla extract.

4. Combine Dry Ingredients:

    - In a separate bowl, whisk together the flour, baking soda, ground cinnamon, and salt.

5. Add Dry Ingredients to Wet Ingredients:

    - Gradually add the dry ingredients to the wet ingredients, mixing until just combined.

6. Fold in Oats and Raisins:

- Fold in the old-fashioned oats and raisins until evenly distributed throughout the cookie dough.

7. Chill Dough (Optional):
   - For enhanced flavor and texture, you can chill the cookie dough in the refrigerator for about 30 minutes to 1 hour.

8. Scoop and Drop Cookies:
   - Drop rounded tablespoons of dough onto the prepared baking sheets, spacing them about 2 inches apart.

9. Bake:
   - Bake in the preheated oven for 10-12 minutes or until the edges are golden but the centers are still soft.

10. Cool on Baking Sheets:
    - Allow the cookies to cool on the baking sheets for 5 minutes before transferring them to wire racks to cool completely.

11. Store:
    - Once cooled, store the oatmeal raisin cookies in an airtight container at room temperature.

12. Enjoy:
    - Enjoy these classic oatmeal raisin cookies with a glass of milk or your favorite beverage.

Feel free to customize these cookies by adding nuts, using different types of raisins, or incorporating other mix-ins like chocolate chips. Oatmeal raisin cookies are a timeless favorite that brings warmth and nostalgia to any occasion.

www.ingramcontent.com/pod-product-compliance
Lightning Source LLC
LaVergne TN
LVHW081555060526
838201LV00054B/1890